Birhanu

Employee Retention M

Birhanu Gebresilassie Girma

Employee Retention Management Strategy

Basics

LAP LAMBERT Academic Publishing

Impressum/Imprint (nur für Deutschland/only for Germany)
Bibliografische Information der Deutschen Nationalbibliothek: Die Deutsche Nationalbibliothek verzeichnet diese Publikation in der Deutschen Nationalbibliografie; detaillierte bibliografische Daten sind im Internet über http://dnb.d-nb.de abrufbar.
Alle in diesem Buch genannten Marken und Produktnamen unterliegen warenzeichen-, marken- oder patentrechtlichem Schutz bzw. sind Warenzeichen oder eingetragene Warenzeichen der jeweiligen Inhaber. Die Wiedergabe von Marken, Produktnamen, Gebrauchsnamen, Handelsnamen, Warenbezeichnungen u.s.w. in diesem Werk berechtigt auch ohne besondere Kennzeichnung nicht zu der Annahme, dass solche Namen im Sinne der Warenzeichen- und Markenschutzgesetzgebung als frei zu betrachten wären und daher von jedermann benutzt werden dürften.

Coverbild: www.ingimage.com

Verlag: LAP LAMBERT Academic Publishing GmbH & Co. KG
Heinrich-Böcking-Str. 6-8, 66121 Saarbrücken, Deutschland
Telefon +49 681 3720-310, Telefax +49 681 3720-3109
Email: info@lap-publishing.com

Herstellung in Deutschland:
Schaltungsdienst Lange o.H.G., Berlin
Books on Demand GmbH, Norderstedt
Reha GmbH, Saarbrücken
Amazon Distribution GmbH, Leipzig
ISBN: 978-3-8473-1661-9

Imprint (only for USA, GB)
Bibliographic information published by the Deutsche Nationalbibliothek: The Deutsche Nationalbibliothek lists this publication in the Deutsche Nationalbibliografie; detailed bibliographic data are available in the Internet at http://dnb.d-nb.de.
Any brand names and product names mentioned in this book are subject to trademark, brand or patent protection and are trademarks or registered trademarks of their respective holders. The use of brand names, product names, common names, trade names, product descriptions etc. even without a particular marking in this works is in no way to be construed to mean that such names may be regarded as unrestricted in respect of trademark and brand protection legislation and could thus be used by anyone.

Cover image: www.ingimage.com

Publisher: LAP LAMBERT Academic Publishing GmbH & Co. KG
Heinrich-Böcking-Str. 6-8, 66121 Saarbrücken, Germany
Phone +49 681 3720-310, Fax +49 681 3720-3109
Email: info@lap-publishing.com

Printed in the U.S.A.
Printed in the U.K. by (see last page)
ISBN: 978-3-8473-1661-9

This Work is dedicated to My Mother, **Muluemebet Getu and all my Families**

i

ery, his cheerful
support in arranging overall financial and non financial support as well as nonstop encouragement
happened to be greatly instrumental for immersing myself in the foreseeable research undertakings.
Furthermore, Special cooperation and support was secured from respondents and employees of Dashen
Brewery. Particulary, Ato Zewudu Gebeyhu , Ato H/Mariam Assefa, Ato Gezahagn Yadete, Ato Asfaw
Tilahun, Ato Gashawu Teklie, and W/ro Mesert all appeard keen and firmly stood by my side while
collecting data.

I highly appreciate and thank to Professor Eshetu Woncheko (PhD) and Professor Trusew Tefera(PhD)
who were cooperative and helpful in sharing their precious experience related to research and use of
statistical tools.

 I also indebted to Daba Gadissa and my heart also could not escape without thanking Adamu Kebede
(General Manger, Beles Consulting Plc) who supported and encouraged me to succeed in my academic
progress; and could always be counted for their support, courage and   motivation.
 I am also grateful to Solomon Alebel and Eshetie Berhan for their continuous support and encouragement
to accomplish this task on time.

Last but not the least my sincere thank and deep appreciation is extended to my best friends ; Mahir Jibril,
Dargie Arbssie and Girma Belete who provided guidance and direction in all academic matters and
always they are unique in creating and formulating sound solutions for problems in team discussion/
round tables.

Birhanu G/Silassie

ii

Table of Content

Contents	Page No.

Chapter one

Chapter Two

Chapter Three

Chapter Four

Chapter five

List of tables

List of figures

Abstract

Employee retention is one of the challenges facing many business organizations today. For many organizations, strategic staffing has become a concern because the ability to hold on highly talented core employees can be crucial to future survival. This project examined the employee retention strategy of Dashen Brewery PLC. In particular, the research identified the core elements of HRM and organizational factors, which strongly influence the decision for employees to stay.

These specific factors consisted of two bundles of practices: HR factors (e.g., person organizational fit, remuneration, reward and recognition, training and career development, challenging job opportunities) and Organizational factors (e.g., leadership behavior, company culture and policies, teamwork relationship and satisfactory work environment). The outcome of the HRM-retention relationship was examined through organizational commitment and turnover intention using correlation and multiple regression analysis. The findings of this study revealed positive significant co- relationships between the eight factors and organizational commitment and intention to stay. Moreover, it was highlighted that commitment acted as a partial mediator of remuneration, recognition and reward, training and career development and work environment on intent to stay.

Another findings of the study demonstrates that commitment can be influenced by bundles of HR factors (i.e. selection (person organization fit), remuneration, reward and recognition, training and career development, challenging assignments) and Organizational factors (i.e. leadership behavior, organizational culture and policies, teamwork relationship and satisfactory work environment.) Moreover, commitment acts as a partial mediator of the relationship between remuneration, recognition and reward, training and career development and work environment on intent to stay. Commitment fully mediates the relationship between person organization fit, teamwork relationship, culture and policies and intention to stay.

This study sought to identify factors that affect employee retention and predict ways that the company can improve on current practices. The study is a step toward understanding employee retention problems, but should not be seen as a final answer. Staff members are unique which means that continued research and analysis is needed to improve employee retention rates at Dashen Brewery.

List of Acronyms

AAU....................Addis Ababa University

ANRS..................Amhara National Regional State

DB...................... Dashen Brewery

DV......................Dependent variable

ID.......................Independent variable

EOC....................Employer of Choice

ERS....................Employee Retention Strategy

ET......................Employee Turn over

HRF....................Human Resource Factors

HRM...................Human Resource Management

KSA....................Knowledge, Skill and Ability

SPSS...................Statistical Package for social science

TI.......................Turnover Intention

Key words: *Employees, HR-factors, Organizational factors, organizational commitment,*
turnover intention, and employee retention

Chapter one

Introduction

Organizations today constantly wrestle with revolutionary trends: accelerating product and technological changes, global competition, deregulation, demographic changes, and at the same time, they must strive to implement trends towards a service and information age society (Kane 2000). Due to this tumultuous business environment, one of the challenges facing many business organizations is the retention of employees. Society has now become knowledge- based where clearly human capital is considered a key resource and indispensable- to the survival of businesses. Increasingly, organizations are competing for the best talented employees (Porter 2001).

For many organizations strategic staffing has become an important issue because the ability to hold on to highly talented employees can be crucial to future survival (Ibid). The loss of needed talent is costly because of the resultant bidding up of market salaries for experienced hirees to replace them; the costs of recruiting and assimilating new talent; the lost investment in talent development; and the hidden costs of lost productivity; lost sales opportunities; and strained customer relationships (Eskildsen and Nussler, 2000). Statistics show that; the cost of replacing an employee usually amounts to a quarter of an individual's annual salary (Ibid). A company with 50,000 employees incurs replacement costs approaching $18 million a year (Ibid).

According to a study released by Accenture (2001), 80 percent of global business leaders believe that 'people issues' were more important than they had been three years before, and 68 percent believe that retaining talent was more important than acquiring 'new blood'. That recognition and the extraordinary efforts some companies are making to attract and retain top talent represent fundamental shifts in employer-employee relationships.

1

Essentially more organizations are now realizing that retention is a strategic issue and represents a competitive advantage (Walker 2001).

As the retention of talent with critical skill sets is acknowledged by organizations as vital for the achievement of business growth and the building of organizational competencies, some organizations strive to be the 'employer of choice' by creating a positive environment and offering challenging assignments that foster continued personal growth. An 'employer of choice' (EOC) is an organization that outperforms its competition in the attraction, development and retention of people with business-required aptitude, often through innovative and compelling human resource programs (Clarke 2001).

In today's business environment employees appear to be less committed to their respective organizations. An employer cannot guarantee the stability and longevity of corporate career paths or the security of employees' jobs (Kane 2000). The old contract of employee loyalty in exchange for job security and fair work has broken down. The trend, these days, seems to be geared towards having a 'career portfolio' (Kane 2000). It is important to note that employees today realize that they have to take the initiative in job resiliency, developing the skills and flexibility needed to quickly respond to shifting employer requirements (Beck 2001).

Overall, powerful and unstable market forces have overwhelmed non-market institutional structures, resulting in decreased employee commitment and increased flexibility of employment. However, this increased flexibility for employers coincides with decreasing tenure and job instability for workers. The use of these non-standard employment arrangements may have long term consequences. Flexibility may be good business for the employer, but in many cases it may be devastating for the worker. Employment instability is contributing to the growing inequality in income, status, and economic security in the country.

As workers face a pace of change unprecedented in history, and as "empowerment" and the need for risk taking, coupled with longer hours and less leisure time, have increased their risk of 'burnout' tenfold, employees' values have shifted discernibly (Porter 2001).

2

High talent personnel see the greatest opportunities by moving from one company to another. Increasingly, organizations will have to compete for the best talent. Consequently, this will have a significant impact on' the nature of recruitment and selection, training and development, performance management and retrenchment programs (Ibid).

The Cost of Employee Turnover

Abbasi and Hollman (2000) sought to determine the impact of employee turnover on organizations and found that excessive employee turnover often engenders far-reaching consequences and, at the extreme, may jeopardize efforts to attain organizational objectives. In addition, Abbasi and Hollman (2000) indicated that when an organization loses a critical employee, there is negative impact on innovation, consistency in providing service to guests may be jeopardized, and major delays in the delivery of services to customers may occur. The study also showed that a decline in the standard of service provided to guests could also adversely affect the satisfaction of internal and external customers and consequently, the profitability of the organization.

Examples from prior research reveal the incredible cost incurred in losing critical employees. For example, in one study (Hale,1998), employers cited recruitment costs of 50 to 60% of an employee's first year's salary and up to 100% for certain specialized, high-skill positions. In another study, Fitz-enz (1990) indicated that when direct and indirect costs are combined, the total turnover cost of an exempt employee is a minimum of one year's pay and benefits, or a maximum of two years' pay and benefits As part of the process of developing and implementing strategies to maintain and increase competitiveness, organizations face the challenge of retaining their best employees.

As such, this research was designed to analyze and determine the most effective ways for one employer to retain its critical employees. The company in this study has been maintaining a relatively low turnover ratio, but the employees who left the organization

3

have been critical for the company, thus presenting a significant challenge. The results of this research effort potentially could be used as a framework for guiding employee retention in other similar companies also. Employee turnover remains one of the most widely researched topics in organizational analyses (Ibid). Despite significant research progress there still remains a great deal of confusion as to what factors actually cause employeesto leave/remain in their organizations. Among those factors are the external factors (the labour market); institutional factors (such as physical working conditions, pay, job skill, supervision and so on); employee personal characteristics (such as intelligence and aptitude, personal history, sex, interests, age, length of service and so on) and employee's reaction to his/her job (including aspects such as job satisfaction, job involvement and job expectations) (Ibid).

Despite the substantial literature on HRM "best practices and high performance practices," there is however, little consensus among researchers with regard to precisely which HRM practices should be stay. Results from this study will assist in the development of HRM system that will work to combat attrition. Given these different approaches to HRM, it is evident that a more consolidated field of investigation would be beneficial to the development of knowledge in this area. Essentially, it is the need to address this situation that has led to statement of problem.

By adopting an effective total retention strategy with the support of relevant HR programs, businesses may successfully keep employees. The area of the project was selected with the discussion made with the managements of Dashen brewery. This research examines the management practice on the retention of employees in Dashen brewery. It explores the relationship between human resource (HR) practices and retention and further identifies the elements of HR practices which strongly influence the decision for employees to stay. Without valuable employees, a business cannot generate revenue and prosper. Every individual have a purpose to perform and without single one, the picture becomes invisible to be successful in real manner. Retaining the employees is the most important target for the organization because sometimes the high salary or the designation is not important for the employee to stay in the organization. The results from the study may assist in the development of an effective HRM retention program for organizations. More over the project will identify possible reasons of employee turnover and provide possible solutions.

Purpose of the Work

The aim of this study is to investigate and determine the current human resource practices on the retention of employees in Dashen Brewery plc. It will examine the relationship between HR and organizational factors with retention and further identify the elements of HR and organizational factors, which strongly influence the decision for employees to stay. Results from this study will assist in the development of an effective HRM retention program for the company. Employee retention is a highly important strategic tool for companies. It may improve employers' chances of selecting employees who will become committed to their organization and also improve their ability to retain highly skilled and motivated employees.

Focus of the work

What are the most influential HRM and Organizational factors in encouraging employees to remain with their organization?

Statement of the problem

With the attention paid to downsizing----------in recent years, few companies have invested time and money in retaining employees. The focus has been on separating employees from the company. However, be it any type of organization, the organization is expected to provide effective and efficient services to the users in its area of operation. In order to do so, various types of resources have been made optimally available and accessible for effective operation of the organization and better competitiveness. As part of the process of developing and implementing strategies to maintain and increase competitiveness, organizations face the challenge of retaining their best employees.

In today's competitive scenario, as the awareness and technology plays a vital role in developing the competition more vigorous and intense. Retention becomes one of the biggest issues for the brewery industry because people are the one who generates profits

5

and considered as the capital or asset of the organization. Brewery is one of the fast growing industries in Ethiopia so the most important thing to make pace with this evolving competition is to work on the most important determinants of employee retention. Employee retention is one of the greatest challenges that Dashen Brewery currently faces. In order to provide high quality services to customers and to maximize its market share and profit, Dashen brewery needs to maintain an adequate number of well trained employees, in all activity areas.

Retention is a voluntary move by an organisation to create an environment which engages employees for a long term (Fit-enz 1997). The main purpose of retention is to prevent the loss of competent employees from leaving the organisation as this could have adverse effect on productivity and profitability. However, retention practices have become a daunting and highly challenging task for managers and Human Resources (HR) practitioners in today's work force.

Fitz-enz (1997) stated that the average company loses approximately $1 million with every 10 managerial and professional employees who leave the organization. As mentioned previously, the combined direct and indirect costs associated with one employee ranges from a minimum of one year's pay and benefits to a maximum of two years' pay and benefits. Thus, there is significant economic impact when an organization loses any of its critical employees, especially given the knowledge that is lost with the employee's departure.

Management scholars argue that how employees are managed is becoming a more important source of competitive advantage because traditional sources (product and process technology, protected or regulated markets, access to financial .resources and economies of scale) are less powerful than they once were (Ibid).

A discussion made with the general manger of the company (Ato Mekbib Alemu), employee turnover was their critical problem more over this; they have faced challenges why employees were quite from their job and what factor/s really determent/s of employee decision to stay or leave .As the General manger said, the average number of employee

6

who leave the company has significant proportion out of the total employees working for the company. As supported by Fitz-enz (1997) above, the company has a horrific trend of employee retention management. This Turnover leads to a variety of costs for Dashen brewery including training new hires, quality of service to clients and decreased morale in the remaining workforce. Training for new hires is a costly process. It also means that the remaining employees must continue to provide services without an adequate number of employees. The increase in workload may lead to job stress, as well as a decrease in the morale of the workforce as a result the company may lose its market share and profitability. Assuming that, the company decides for new recruitment, the new bloods require time to build a relationship with other staff and to internalize the work environment. Recognize the commitment of individuals to the company, as well as the comapny's need to create an environment in which one would be willing to stay.

During this course, the company will need to either create an intellectual capital environment where the transmission of knowledge takes place throughout the structure, or continue to lose important individual knowledge that has been developed during the length of service. This deep knowledge is what many believe will help to meet the needs and expectations of the customers and to create and sustain a competitive advantage within the national market in which Dashen Brewery is competing today.The problem will be clearly identified and remedial actions can be taken with the support of scientific research. Therefore, examining of the retention management practices of the company will be crucial to address what I said before.

For this end, it is imperative to investigate and determine the management of employee retention strategy in Dashen Brewery and also examining the relationship between HR practices and retention. Identify the elements of HR practices, which strongly influence the decision for employees to stay has significant contribution for the company to improve its ability to retain highly skilled and motivated employees. In order to gain better insights into the process and practices that companies utilize to retain their employees, key research questions are formulated to guide the project. The primary research questions that will be addressed by the project have identified as follow:

7

?. *Why do employees leave the company they work for?*

?. *Does Dashen Brewery have proper retention strategy?*

?. *What are the current management practices of the company on employee turnover management?*

?. *What are the causes for employee turnover and what relationship are there between employees' turnover with HR and Organizational Factors?*

?. *What HRM and organizational factor/s influence employees' decisions to stay?*

?. *Which factor/s is/are most influential for the decision of employees to stay?*

?. *What does the upper management team of the brewery believe on the reasons personnel are leaving the company?*

?. *What are the potential problems related to turn over management?*

Significance of the Study

Retaining valuable employees is one of the important issues for competitive organizations today as employees are the most valuable assets in any company. It is usually in a company's best interest to put its energy in retaining the quality employees that they already have, and not recruiting them. However, increasing employee turnover has been a trend in many organizations today and the issue of staff retention has continued to plague for most organizations across the world. A continuing organizational issue for management and human resource personnel has been the retention of high performance employees. The importance of this study is to examine the capability of Dashen Brewery in retaining employees by different determinants. Reducing employee turnover is a strategic and very important issue. No business can enjoy and sustain the success until it deals with this turnover problem efficiently and successfully. Most critical thing is to lay the groundwork for long term commitment.

8

In this regard, the results of this study are significant in various respects. Firstly, on the basis of the findings of the study, the report draws some conclusions and recommendations based on the findings. This conclusion and recommendation will help the company's ability of managing employee turnover and retention for better performance.

It also important to determine the factors that most significantly influence employees' decisions to remain employed at Dashen brewery and possible reasons for choosing to leave. In addition, the study will describe the importance of retaining critical employees and developing strategies to enhance employee retention practices. More over identifying clearly the prevailing problems of retention management in the company will be of paramount importance in getting possible solutions because a problem clearly identified and articulated is half solved. Second, it is a piece of contribution to the current knowledge in the practice of retention management at the brewery industry in Ethiopia and invites for further research in the areas of employee retention and turnover.

Thirdly, it gives the researcher the opportunity to gain deep knowledge on the practice of employee retention management. Generally the project has the following significances; Serve as a base line data for other studies, increase the research pool on the area, give an insight for the concerned bodies, indicate and recommend for possible interventions, and encourage young researchers and companies/organizations to undertake more researches/projects on the area.

Objective of the work

General objective

The intent of this paper will help to find how valuable employees would be retained by focusing on certain determinants. To attract handfuls of people and making huge efforts to make them stay in the company, the discussion will be helpful to know, why employees left the organization and the reason of getting appealed by others. The general objective of the study is to examine Employee Retention management practice/ explore and pinpoint problems and malpractices against HR and organizational factors of Dashen brewery.

9

Specific objectives

Specifically, the study intends to:

➤ *Find out possible cause of employee turnover and the company's retention strategy*

➤ *Investigate the current management practices of the company on employee turnover management*

➤ *Spot which HRM and organizational factor/s influence employees' decisions to stay.*

➤ *Indicate which factor/s is/are the most influential for the decision of employees to stay.*

➤ *Know whether the the upper management team of the brewery believe on the reasons personnel are leaving the company*

➤ *Identify and establish the causes for employee turnover and the relationship between employee turnover with HR and organizational Factors*

➤ *Discover potential problems related to turn over management and suggest possible solution*

Scope of the Work

The purpose of this study will be to determine the factors that most significantly influence employees' decisions to remain employed at Dashen brewery and possible reasons for choosing to leave. In addition, the study will describe the importance of retaining critical employees and developing strategies to enhance employee retention practices. In doing so, the researcher will consider the workers at the factory and precludes other staffs working elsewhere. This report is limited to the data obtained using questionnaires and FGD in the factory in addition to other secondary documents obtained from the company. Regardless of the multifarious characteristics of employee retention strategy, the report is limited to the employees' perception of the problems and practices of retention management.

10

Limitations of the Work

There are many other factors which may affect the level of employee retention but due to time constraint others are not taken into consideration. More over the study population will also be limited to workers at the factory. The accuracy of the results may be influenced by biases. The study is exclusive of any intervening or moderating variables. The response from participants may be lower than expected, which may interfere with their willingness to participate.

Ethical issue

Five ethical issues have been taken into account for the study. These issues are; voluntary participation and informed consent, no harm to participants, anonymity, deceiving subjects, and analyzing and reporting of the research findings. All participation in this research was voluntary and participants of the study were given a full description of the study before deciding to participate. Also, all participants were required to sign informed consent forms before participating. Every effort in this study was guard against harming any research participant. All surveys were kept anonymous/nameless/ for the research. This study was conducted in a straightforward manner and participants in the research were not deceived (misleading). Last, all of the data that is analyzed was reported in this study.

Organization and Reporting of the Work

The project comprises five chapters. Chapter one provides an overview about the back ground of the project. Chapter two concentrates on the research methodology. Chapter three briefs literature related to employee retention, factors that might affect the retention of employees and indicators of turn over intention. And chapter four will provide detail discussions and analysis of the project. Chapter 5 will conclude with a discussion of the major findings , conclusion and recommendation of the study. The final draft of the project was submitted in both hard and soft copy format to Dashen brewery and to the researcher's advisor.

11

Chapter two

Methodology of the project

Study Area

The study was conducted in Dashen Brewery PLC which is found in Amhara National Regional state (ANRS), at the historical town of Gonder. Gonder is located 750 Km away from the capital city of Ethiopia (Addis Ababa) in the North –West.

Research design

Both quantitative and qualitative study design (mixed system approach) was used to assess the significance of HR factors and organizational factors towards employee retention.

Study Population

The study population for this study was all (490) employees working at the factory. These include all management and non management staffs who work in General manger, HR, Marketing, and Supply, Quality assurance, Finance, Production, and Maintenance departments.

Sampling procedure/technique

To estimate single population proportion, the sample size can be determined using formula, if p is not known it has to be taken as 0.5. Depending on the nature of the study 10-15% contingency should be added. If the size of the population is less than 100,000 the sample size should be corrected using the formula as described below(Berenson, et al 1996).

To determine the sample size for this study, it was used an assumption of the margin of error as 0.05 and confidence interval of 95% with the above assumption the sample size was calculated using single population proportion.

$$n= \frac{(Z\alpha/2)^2 \, p \, (1-p)}{d^2} = \frac{(1.96)^2 \, (0.5 \times 0.5)}{0.05^2} = 384$$

> ### Assumption
> o n= sample size
> o Z α /2=1.96 level of significant
> o P=proportion which gives large sample size is 50%
> o d= margin of error 0.05

The sample size is calculated using the following formula.

Therefore, the population proportion for assess factors on employee intention to stay gives large sample size was taken for final sample size calculation in this case p=50 was taken. According to Berenson, et al (1996), since the source population is less than 10,000 correction factor was used. I.e. Corrected sample size = Corrected sample size = $\frac{n \times N}{n+N}$

Where: n is the non-corrected sample size and N is the size of the source population .

Therefore the corrected sample will be = $\frac{384 x 490}{384+490}$ = 215 considering the non response rate as 10% so the total sample size was 237 employees of the factory. The sampling method used to select the study participants for this study was purposive for top managements, cluster sampling for each department and simple random sampling to select regular employees among the cluster. This is to have representative sample, from each departments of Dashen brewery. Coming to FGD, a total twelve participants; i.e. eight top managements, two labour union representatives and two randomly selected employees were participated. The members of the participant will be the general manager, marketing manager, HR department manager, supply department manger; quality assurance department manager, finance department manger, production department manager, maintenance department manger, two labour union representatives, and two employees selected randomly.

Data Collection method

The data collection was done through both primary and secondary sources. The primary data was collected through questionnaire and Focus Group Discussion(FGD). Secondary data was collected from the company's documents and different research papers. The

13

questionnaires were distributed among the employees of Lower, Middle and Upper Level managements of the said departments. The data was collected for 15-days at the factory, Gonder town.

Measuring Instruments

The study measure the relationship of various variables. A co relational analysis was performed using the acquired data, to ascertain the existence of relationship between the variables. For doing the data analysis, Statistical Package for Social Sciences (SPSS version 17) was used, because it is very systematic computer program that can deal with a large amount of data and can give out accurate results. With the help of SPSS, results would be analyzed by tabulating the data using frequency tables, mean, correlation, and regression values.

Measurement of Constructs

The Employee Questionnaire was designed to examine the dependent variable turnover intention. The independent variables were based on eight variables previously identified and validated in. Each independent variable was assessed using a minimum of three items to a maximum of eight items. All items were scored along a five point scale ranging from (1) strongly disagree to (5) strongly agree (Likert 1961). Scales used in previous research was employed to measure the independent and dependent variables of the study.

Data Collection Process

An employee self-completion questionnaire was the instrument employed in this study. This study identified nine factors that influence retention of employees. These were person-organization fit (selection), remuneration and recognition, training and career development, challenging assignment, leadership behavior, team relationship, communication and consultation, company culture (i.e. vision, mission, objectives and values), policies , and work environment. Organizational commitment and turnover intention were the outcomes examined.

14

The questionnaire was designed to allow the researcher to collect the relevant information to test the proposed model. Sixty questions were incorporated into the questionnaire for the purpose of this study. A copy of the original questionnaire is provided in Appendix A. Five questions were used to obtain demographic information on gender, age, qualification, department, and Experience. The remaining fifty-five questions measured the following variables:

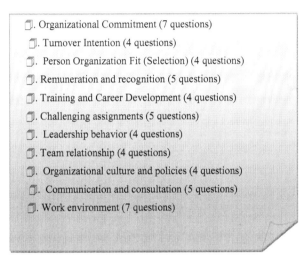

□. Organizational Commitment (7 questions)

□. Turnover Intention (4 questions)

□. Person Organization Fit (Selection) (4 questions)

□. Remuneration and recognition (5 questions)

□. Training and Career Development (4 questions)

□. Challenging assignments (5 questions)

□. Leadership behavior (4 questions)

□. Team relationship (4 questions)

□. Organizational culture and policies (4 questions)

□. Communication and consultation (5 questions)

□. Work environment (7 questions)

The eight department employees of the company participated in this study. Based on the calculation under the sampling procedure, A total of 75 questionnaires were distributed with 74 returned, indicating a response rate of 98.3 percent. This was deemed a good sample size (Comrey and Lee 1992). Hence, the sample size of the study was deemed suitable.

Measures of Reliability

Reliability refers to the degree to which measures are free from random error and therefore yield consistent results (Zikmund 1997). The scales of the eleventh factorized variables were checked for reliability using Cronbach's Alpha using SPSS version 17.0. The results of the tests for each scale (11) are shown in the Table 1.

15

Table 1: Reliability statistics

Variables	Cronbach's alphas	N of items
Person Organization Fit (Selection)	0.587	4
Remuneration and recognition	0.779	5
Training and Career Development	0.751	4
Challenging assignments	0. 787	5
Leadership behavior	0.915	4
Team relationship	0.758	4
Organizational culture and policies	0.835	4
Communication and consultation	0.793	5
Work environment	0.798	7
Organizational Commitment	0.799	9
Turnover Intention	0.803	4
Mean	0.711	

An alpha of 0.70 or above is considered to be reliable as suggested by many researchers (Davis 1996). Apart from the person organization fit scale (=0.587), the Cronbach's alphas for all other scales in the study were judged to be reliable (=>0.7) (Hair *et al.* 1992).

The items of measurement for person organization fit (selection) and the items of measurement for organizational commitment were shown to have common characteristics (indication of overlapping in factor analysis). This may have affected the reliability of the person organization fit scale because it lacked discriminating power.

Data Analysis

The statistical package for the social sciences was used to analyze the quantitative data (SPSS for Windows version 17.0). Initially, all items were reversed coded from "1" to "5", "0" to "1", and "1" to "8" and so on. The eleven variables were screened for normality by

16

examining kurtosis and skewness value. Most often, variables conform to normal distribution. The distributions are usually skewed (negative or positive) and display varying degrees of kurtosis (positive or negative). Summaries of the data were undertaken, including frequency percentage distribution, mean and standard deviation. The statistical analyses used included correlation, reliabilities, and multiple regressions.

For this study, the primary goal of the regression analysis is to investigate the relationship between the dependent variable (DV) and several independent variables (IVs) and test the hypothesis of the study. The regression model selected for this study is the stepwise regression used to develop a group of independent variables that is useful in predicting the dependent variables and to eliminate those independent variables that do not provide any additional prediction to the independent variables already in the equation (Tabachnick and Fidell 2001).

Missing data: When there are a few data points missing in a random pattern from the data set, it was discarded. All missing data will be rejected from further analysis.

Means, and standard deviations and correlations

Correlation coefficients were calculated for initial exploration of the relationships between variables. Correlation is used to measure the size and direction of the relationship between two variables (Tabachnick and Fidell 2001). In this study, a correlation analysis was carried out to measure the inter-relationship between independent variables (person organization fit, remuneration and recognition, training and career development, challenging assignments, leadership behavior, teamwork relationship, company culture and policies, work environment), dependent variables (organizational commitment and intention to stay) and the demographic information (sex and qualification).

On completion of the correlation analysis, a regression analysis was conducted in order to further evaluate and understand the relationships between the dependent and independent variables of the study, and to test the hypotheses of interest.

Multiple Regression Analysis

The regression model selected for this study is stepwise regression and the dependent variables examined were organizational commitment and intent to stay (Turnover intention). The purpose of stepwise regression analysis was to develop a group of independent variables that are useful in predicting the dependent variables and to eliminate those independent variables that do not provide any additional prediction to the independent variables already in the equation (Tabachnick and Fidell 2000).

In this study, the stepwise regression analysis was conducted to test the relationship between the eight independent variables of the study: person organization fit, remuneration and recognition, training and career development, challenging assignments, leadership, teamwork, policies, and work environment and the dependent variables: Commitment and Intent to stay (Turnover Intention). Sex and qualification were the demographic factors included as control variables. Age, department, and experience were excluded because the correlation matrix indicated insignificant relationships (Appendix B).

Chapter Three

Literature Review and Conceptual framework

This chapter describes the relationship between human resource and organizational factors with the retention of employees. It examines the causes of poor employee commitment and specifically explores relevant literature to identify elements of HR practices that influence employee retention. The related literature is presented in this chapter to provide an overview of the areas covered in the study.

Literature review

Over the past decade, the way in which people are managed and developed at work has come to be recognized as one of the primary factors in achieving improvement in organizational performance (Marchington and Wilkinson 1997). This is reflected by popular idioms such as 'people are our most important asset' (Accenture 2001).

From the review of the extant literature, it is acknowledged that successful organizations share a fundamental philosophy of valuing and investing in their employees (Anand 1997). In fact several research studies have described human resource management as a means of achieving competitive advantage (Delery 1998; Walker 2001). Consistent with this perspective, is an equally important issue for organizations, the retention of their critical (core) employees.

Most organizations today continue to struggle with retention because they are relying on salary increases and bonuses to prevent turnover (Accenture 2001). Essentially, more organizations are now realizing that retention is a strategic issue and represents a competitive advantage (Walker 2001).

Human Resource Management Practices

Basically, employees perform the essential tasks within the organization, and organizational human resource systems are designed to support and manage this human

19

capital (Gramm and Schnell 2001).Current HRM thinking emphasizes the benefits of meeting employee needs and enabling workers to have control over their work lives. Many firms recognize the necessity to provide the information, flexibility and voice that employees require to contribute to organizational success (Becker and Huselid 1998).

Academic research conducted at the organizational level supports that human resource practices affect organizational outcomes by shaping employee behaviors and attitudes (Arthur1994). Ostroff and Bowen (2000) found that human resource practices shape work force attitudes by molding employees' perceptions of what the organization is like and influencing their expectations of the nature and depth of their relationship with the organization. There is also a general notion that human resource practices interact with perceptions of organizational support to affect employee commitment.

More specifically, systems of "high commitment" human resource practices increase organizational effectiveness by creating conditions where employees become highly involved in the organization and work hard to accomplish the organization's goals (Arthur 1994). Many managers today recognize the benefits of "high commitment" human resource management practices that respond to employees' needs, encourage employees to take responsibility for their work lives, and motivate employees to behave in ways that benefit the organization. Information sharing, open channels of communication, extensive training, and incentive compensation are some of the practices consistently found in this "high commitment" category (Ibid).

Lawler (1992) describe high commitment HRM as "an ensemble of HR practices that aim at getting more from workers by giving more to them" (p. 189). "High commitment" practices are those that make it easier for employees to take responsibility for their own work lives as they contribute to organizational goals. Employees are more pivotal in a high-involvement organization because such a firm is employee-centered by design; information and decision-making power are dispersed throughout the organization, with employees at all levels taking on greater responsibility for its operation and success. To facilitate this approach, high-involvement organizations use human resource practices that develop and support a workforce that is self-programming and self-managing (Lawler 1992). A number

20

of texts have appeared in recent years promoting the advantages of using high-involvement or high-commitment human resource practices, a system of human resources practices thought to enhance employees' levels of skill, motivation, information, and empowerment (Ibid).

The extensive use of high-involvement work practices represents a significant investment in human capital. Basic microeconomics suggests that investments in human capital (employees) are justified when such investments are more than offset by future returns in the form of increased productivity. Thus, firms will make greater use of such practices when employees are viewed as particularly vital to firm success (Barney 1991).

With respect to retaining these critical human assets, greater use of high-involvement work practices is likely to have two broad implications. First, previous work (Arthur 1994) indicated that high-involvement work practices will enhance employee retention. At the same time, there is also the argument that the greater use of high-involvement work practices will increase the cost of employee departures. This is consistent with the resource-based view of the firm. From this perspective, firms can achieve sustainable competitive advantage by creating value in a rare and inimitable manner (Barney 1991). However, because the use of these practices increases the uniqueness and value of employees, it will also increase the costs associated with the loss of these employees.

In a study of over 900 organizations in the United States, Huselid (1995) suggested that human resource practice be grouped into two categories: those practices that improve employee skills and those that enhance employee motivation. This study found that skill-enhancing human resource activities included selection and training activities and were associated with turnover and financial performance, and that motivation-enhancing activities included performance appraisal and compensation activities and were associated with measures of productivity. The common theme is utilizing a system of management practices giving employees skills, information, motivation and latitude, resulting in a workforce that is a source of competitive advantage.

21

Most strategic HRM researchers have tended to take a holistic view of employment and human capital, focusing on the extent to which a set of practices is used across all employees of a firm as well as the consistency of these practices across all employees (Pfeffer 1994) They suggest that there is an identifiable set of best practices for managing employees that has universal, additive, positive effects on organizational performance (universalistic approach). The contingency approach differs from the universalistic perspective in that the studies have attempted to link HRM systems and the complementarily of variations of HRM practices to specific organizational strategies (Arthur 1994).

Similar to the contingency approach, the configurational approach argues that fit of HRM practices with organizational strategy is a vital factor in the HRM-firm performance relationship (Becker and Gerhart 1996). However, the configurational approach takes this argument a step further in asserting that there are specific "ideal types" of HRM systems that provide both horizontal and vertical fit of HRM practices to organizational structure and strategic goals. Delery and Doty (1996) identified seven practices consistently considered to be "strategic" in nature. Practices identified were internal career opportunities, formal training systems, appraisal measures, profit sharing, employment security, voice mechanisms and job definition. Pfeffer (1994), however, advocated the use of sixteen management practices to achieve higher productivity and profits.

The practices that represent a high commitment strategy include sets of organization-wide human resource policies and procedures that affect employee commitment and motivation. Arthur (1994) found very strong correlations between employee retention and productivity in high-commitment HR systems. The identified HR practices included selective staffing, developmental appraisal, competitive and equitable compensation, and comprehensive training and development activities (Snell and Dean 1992). These human resource practices can be classified as "control" or "commitment" practices (Arthur 1994). Control approaches aim to increase efficiency and reduce direct labour costs and rely on strict work rules and procedures and base rewards on outputs (Arthur 1994). Rules, sanctions, rewards and monitoring regulate employee behavior (Ibid)

22

The preceding arguments of set of practices also support the concept of "bundles" of HR practices. A bundle of interrelated, overlapping HR practices provides several ways for workers to acquire skills (for example, off-the-job and on-the-job training, job rotation, problem-solving groups) and multiple incentives to boost motivation (for example, extrinsic rewards such as performance-based pay and intrinsic rewards from participating in decision-making and good job design) (Lawson & Hepp 2000). Therefore, innovative human resource practices affect performance not individually but as interrelated elements in an internally consistent HR "bundle" or system (MacDuffie 1995). There is now ample empirical support for the bundling or systems view (Ibid).

Human Resource Management Factors influencing retention

There is growing evidence that human resource management can play an important role in retaining a high-quality workforce. Studies of progressive HRM practices in training, compensation and reward sharing have revealed that these can lead to reduced turnover and absenteeism, better quality work, and better financial performance (Arthur 1994).

Furthermore, an extensive study (Accenture 2001) on high performance issues identified the retention strategies of organizations primarily from US, Europe, Asia and Australia. These strategies included the following: offering comprehensive training and development—to all staff, be it permanent, part-time or contract, allowing staff to work on project-based assignments, broadening their skills whist keeping them challenged and interested in their work,   empowering and entrusting staff with responsibility, ensuring that a balance exists between work and lifestyle, and that the culture is such that it supports this philosophy, providing flexible work arrangements, connecting staff by means of mentors or coaches, ensuring staff know where they stand with regular performance appraisals, skills development programs and clear career paths embracing emerging technologies, ensuring an effective management style, ensuring good relationships are formed and nurtured with "the boss" aligning people strategies with business strategies providing employee benefits such a social clubs, financial services, providing free career advice, life insurance, fitness and health options rewarding staff well offering competitive salaries.

23

According to Fitz-enz (1990), retention management of employees is influenced by several key factors, which should be managed congruently: organizational culture and structure, recruitment strategy, pay and benefits philosophy, employee support programs, and a training and career development system.

Consequently, organizations utilize a wide range of these HRM factors driving retention and commitment (Ibid). For the purpose of this study, these factors are reviewed and categorized into HR factors (person organization fit, remuneration, training and career development, challenging opportunities) and organizational factors (leadership behavior, teamwork relationship, company culture and policies and satisfactory work environment).

Person Organization Fit (Selection)

The concept of person-job (P-J) fit emphasizes matching people and jobs in terms of qualifications based on knowledge, skill, or ability, and overlooking other personal characteristics of applicants that might be more suitable for the assessment of "fit.". However, as the complexity of work increases, organizations now use more selection methods that capture the applicant's capability to do the work. Research on person-job fit has found that workers gravitate to jobs with complexity levels commensurate with their ability. However, selection should also improve fit between the applicant and other aspects of the work such as e.g. personality fit and organization fit (Smith 1994).

Person-organization fit is considered in the context of personnel selection and can be based on the congruity between personal and organization beliefs or individual and company goals (Smith 1997). The concept of organizational fit identifies convergent goals and values between the individual and the organization as an important element to *affective commitment (Ibid)*. Organization fit as an individual's willingness to cooperate in an organization as cohesion and proposed that "its immediate cause is the disposition necessary to 'sticking together" (p, 84). Selection should therefore consider improving fit between an applicant's values and the organization culture (Ibid).

Lee, et al (1992) found that both person-job fit and person-organization fit predicted job

24

satisfaction; however, person-organization fit was a better predictor of intention to quit. Thus, people who are not well suited for the job and/or organization are more likely to leave than those who have a good person-job or person-organization fit. The organization should not only match the job requirements with the person's knowledge, skills and abilities, but should also carefully match the person's personality and values with the organization's values and culture. Espoused the theory that states an employee's satisfaction with a job, as well as propensity to leave that job, depends on the degree to which the individual's personality matches his or her occupational environment.

Many person organization fit studies emphasized the match between people's values and the values of the organization, because values are conceived of as fundamental and relatively enduring (Ibid). In this study, value congruence and person-culture fit are treated as equivalent terms.

Remuneration, reward and recognition of employee value

Compensation is the most critical issue when it comes to attracting and keeping talent (Willis 2000,). A fair wage is the cornerstone of the contractual and implied agreements between employees and employers, the underlying assumption being that money can influence behavior (Ibid). Companies often provide pay packages superior to the market for critical talent. These include special pay premiums, stock options, or bonuses. Base pay reflects fair pay; supplemental programs reflect individual, team or organizational performance and success.   "Leading edge" firms, defined as firms that use high performance work practices such as total quality management and training, provide innovative compensation such as profit sharing and group-based incentive pay (Ibid).

Organizations in most industries are implementing innovative compensation approaches to differentiate themselves (Parker and Wright 2001). Innovative practices reflect the individual player contract model, focusing on "what it will take" to attract and retain each individual, regardless of the pay of others. This "let's make a deal" approach is a radical departure from traditional pay equity approaches, but seems to work in a highly competitive, individualized talent market. Others act more broadly, ensuring that all

25

"players" are paid near the top of the market, whether through base salary or bonuses (Ibid).

This raises overall compensation costs but may reduce the risk, and therefore the cost, of attrition. Wages influence the recruitment and retention of workers (Parker and Wright 2001) and therefore play a role in the staffing process. However, these studies recognize that pay, by itself, will not be enough to retain people. Low pay will often drive employees out the door, but high pay will not necessarily keep them. Ultimately, they stay because they like their co-workers and are engaged and challenged by work that makes them better at what they do.

Pay continues to be important in determining motivation to perform. Past motivational theories such as expectancy and equity theories have predicted variations in motivation as a result of varying valences of outcomes as pay (Ibid). However, in practice, pay is treated as just one of the outcomes and often measured with little precision. Although an association exists between compensation satisfaction and commitment and is one of the drivers of organization commitment, nevertheless, it has to be considered as one of the pieces in a complex picture (Parker and Wright 2001). Just as important is the organization's need to communicate its total compensation package to its employees. It must emphasize not only the salary, bonuses and benefits, but other highly valued aspects of employment such as supporting life style balance initiatives and flexible work arrangements. These are non-monetary benefits known as intrinsic rewards and they have a significant role in compensation satisfaction (Ibid).

Employees will stay if they are rewarded. Employees are usually rewarded based on quality based performance. A sense of accomplishment is recognized as important and a strong motivator. Employees tend to remain with the organization when they feel their capabilities, efforts and performance contributions are recognized and appreciated (Davies 2001).

Employers are increasing their commitment to the use of rewards as essential elements of talent management programs. It is increasingly important for companies to use their reward

26

budget effectively to differentiate the rewards of the top performers, thus driving an increase in the return on investment (ROI) on human capital investments. The alternatives are decreased employee performance or the attrition of key performers to competitors in an increasingly competitive environment. Thus companies that are committed to their employees typically invest more than similar firms in progressive HRM practices such as training and education, and in the total package of compensation (Arthur 1994).

They also distribute rewards more equitably and generously. Compensation provides recognition, but other forms of non-monetary recognition are also important. Recognition from managers, team members, peers and customers enhance commitment (Walker 2001). Particularly important to the employees are opportunities to participate and to influence actions and decisions (Davies 2001).

There is study that have highlighted the rewards-retention link (Mercer 2003) and provided insights into what employers are doing, how they feel, and what employees have to say on the rewards issue. Mercer's Human Resource study measured the return on reward investments of 302 companies. The research assessed the effectiveness of specific reward and identified the reward program issues and challenges confronting US companies. Mercer's findings indicate that most companies are increasing their focus on attracting and retaining top talent.

Training and career development

Training is considered a form of human capital investment whether that investment is made by the individual or by the firm (Arthur 1994). Once employees are hired, training programs enhance employee job skills. Employees are expected to acquire new skills and knowledge, apply them on the job, and share them with other employees (Noe 1999).

Training provides employees with specific skills or helps to correct deficiencies in their performances; while development is an effort to provide employees with abilities the organization will need in the future (Noe 1999). Skill development could include improving basic literacy, technological know-how, interpersonal communication, or problem solving abilities. Employees want good training opportunities to increase their

27

marketability. The conventional wisdom used to be that if the company makes them marketable, employees will leave at the first opportunity. But today, companies are finding that the more training employees get, the more likely they are to stay. Indeed, when the training ends, the turnover tends to begin (Ibid).

A firm has the incentive to invest in the human capital of its workers only if there is an expectation of a return on its investment. Increasingly, companies are strengthening development for talent, thorough competency analysis, input on individual interests, multi-source assessment of capabilities and development needs, and the formulation of action plans (Clarke 2001).

Training is a symbol of the employer's commitment to staff. It is also reflective of an organizational strategy based on adding value rather than lowering cost. Leading companies have acknowledged that providing employees with a comprehensive range of career and skills-development opportunities is the key to attracting and retaining the kind of flexible, technologically-sophisticated workforce that companies need to succeed in the digital economy. The training and development of people at work has increasingly come to be recognized as an important part of HRM (Ibid).

Level of employee turnover and training are expected to be inversely related: the higher the level of turnover, the lower the amount of training. This expectation is based on the reasoning that the longer an employee stays with an employer; the higher will be the return to training. A recent study by Frazis *et al* (1998) indicated that employees working in low-turnover establishments spent about 59 percent of their total training time in formal training, compared with 18 percent for employees in high-turnover establishments. From the employee's view, if the training involves skills specific to the establishment, it is likely to contribute to an increase in productivity at that establishment. Greater productivity at the establishment, in turn, will tend to raise a worker's wage above what he or she would earn elsewhere, thus providing an incentive to stay. In other words, training can serve to lower turnover (Ibid).

28

Challenging employment assignment and opportunities

Employees need to be stimulated with creative challenges or they will go where the excitement is, be it another department, industry or company. Companies are countering this by allowing employees to choose what projects they want to work on and allowing cross-departmental and cross-disciplinary migration (Accenture 2001). Providing employees with challenging assignments with well-defined performance measures and feedback is important for a high performance environment in which employees can achieve their personal objectives. The necessity of mastering new skills keeps employees satisfied and creative (Walker 2001). Employees want a job with broad duties and a lot of task variety. In part, it is because they want to have more job skills on their resume when they are forced to get another job (Ibid).

A further extension of these efforts to provide job challenges is cross-functional career development. This technique allows the long-term employees which the organization views as having overall leadership potential to move from one area of the company where they have succeeded (e.g., management) to another area where they have no experience (e.g., acquisitions). Moving high-calibre employees in this manner not only assures that they will be challenged, but begins to build employees with enough breadth of experience to assume senior leadership roles with the organization. General Electric and IBM have been doing this for years (Ibid).

Employees who felt that the organization failed to give them challenging and interesting work, freedom to be creative, opportunities to develop new skills, and autonomy and control were more likely to express negativity and lack of loyalty toward their employer. More specifically, when the promises related to autonomy and growth and rewards and opportunities were breached, an employee was more likely to report negative feelings and attitudes toward the organization, lower levels of commitment, and greater intentions to leave the organization (Phillips 1997).

29

Organizational Factors influencing retention

Leadership

Leadership is defined as the behavior of an individual that results in non-coercive influence when that person is directing and coordinating the activities of a group toward the accomplishment of a shared goal (Bryman1992). Leadership is conceptualized in terms of four tasks that need to be accomplished in any organization: providing direction, assuring alignment, building commitment and facing adaptive challenges Leaders are central to the process of creating cultures, systems and structures that foster knowledge creation, sharing and cultivation (Ibid).

Research findings suggested that leadership enhanced organizational commitment (Allen 1996). Though there are differences between the transformational and charismatic leadership theories, scholars are now viewing them as sharing much in common and referring to this body of work as the "new leadership" theory (Ibid).

Transformational leaders are regarded as active leaders that have four distinguishing characteristics: charisma, inspiration, intellectual stimulation and individualized consideration .Numerous leadership studies in a wide variety of organizations have examined the impact of transformational and charismatic leaders, and findings indicate that transformational and charismatic leadership styles "result in a high-level of follower motivation and commitment as well as well-above-average organizational performance (Ibid).

Furthermore, several studies have identified high levels of peak performance under transformational leadership, high correlation between charismatic leadership and effectiveness. Transformational leadership more highly related to employees' perceived satisfaction and effectiveness than transactional leadership (Yammarino and Bass 1990).

Several researchers have highlighted the positive influence of transformational leaders in organizational outcomes which resulted in lowered intention to leave and increased organizational behavior and lead to stronger organizational commitment. Therefore, based

30

on the literature review, it appears that leadership behavior has a positive influence on organizational commitment and turnover intention (Ibid).

Company culture and structure (Policies)

Corporate culture is described as the invisible forces that shape life in a business organization. Management philosophy and style, communications protocol and policies, rituals and taboos interact to create the uniqueness of each company. People often join a company or seek employment within a particular industry because they find its culture appealing (Fitz-enz 1990). However, in the past decade the cultural characteristics of some industries and, therefore, the companies within them have changed markedly. And when the culture changes, whether through growth, new management or economic and regulatory interventions, some people become uncomfortable and leave to find a culture that fits them better (Ibid).

The complement of culture is structure, which is shaped by culture and technology. Structure starts with job design and workflow patterns, and includes policies and procedures, spans of control, reporting relationships and other factors that dictate how work is to be done and business conducted. Both Dashen Brewery and BGI-Ethiopia are producing and selling of beers.

Advocates of strategic cultural change typically make a number of implicit assumptions. First, organizations possess discernible cultures, which affect quality and performance. Second, although cultures may be resistant to change, they are to some extent malleable and manageable. Third, it is possible to identify particular cultural attributes that facilitate or inhibit good performance, and it should therefore be feasible for managers to design strategies for cultural change. Finally, it is assumed that any benefits accruing from the change will outweigh any dysfunctional consequences. Employee commitment may be fostered by employer-employee relationships that allow the accomplishment of corporate financial goals as well as cater to employee needs (Allen 1996).

Research has shown that employees' commitment to an organization affects how well the organization performs in various ways. If it turns out that employee commitment varies in

31

certain predictable ways from one cultural pattern to another, organizational development specialists could try to strengthen employee commitment and, therefore, organizational effectiveness by changing the organizational culture. These studies and anecdotal evidence suggest a positive link between strong organizational cultures and employee commitment (Koene *et al* 1997).

Communication and consultation

Effective communication has emerged from the comprehensive literature review as an essential facet of people management be it communication of the organization's goals, vision, strategies and business policies or the communication of facts, and information and data communication structure. Effective communications strengthen employee identification with the company and build trust (Clarke 2001).

For business success, a regular two-way communication, particularly face to face with employees, was identified as an important factor in establishing trust and a feeling of being valued. Essentially, a two way communication is regarded as a core management competency and as a key management responsibility. For example, the management responsibilities for effective communication include (1) ensuring people are briefed on key issues, (2) communicating honestly and as fully as possible on all issues affecting the people, (3) encouraging team members to discuss company issues and give upward feedback and (4) ensuring issues from team members are fed back to senior management and timely replies given. Successful organizations place great emphasis on communication channels that enable people at all levels. Many formal and informal communication mechanisms exist; all designed to foster an environment of open dialogue, shared knowledge and information as well as a trust in an effective upward, downward, lateral and cross functional structure. Regular employee meetings and other updates allow employees to adjust their efforts to support company objectives (Ibid).

Opportunities for feedback give employees an avenue to influence their work and company policies. Grievance procedures provide a more formalized mechanism by which workers can be heard when they are dissatisfied with a decision or outcome. Supervisors and co-workers are therefore principally responsible for communicating role expectations and feedback about role performance. Hence, organizations that carry out effective communications ensure that their internal communications help their employees make the connection between positive aspects of their workplace and effective management policies (Walker 2001).

Team working relationships

Employees stay when they have strong relationships with their work colleagues. Organizations today encourage team building, project assignments involving work with peers, and opportunities for social interaction both on and off the job. One value of team-based organization is the bond they establish among members (Clarke 2001).

Co-worker supportiveness refers to the friendliness of and the extent to which co-workers pay attention to employee comments and concerns. Interactions with co-workers may serve an affective-psychological function by providing emotional support against the stresses of the organization's socialization initiatives and uncertainties of the work setting. In addition, newcomers and incumbents who have co-worker support while experiencing socialization tactics and learning new roles are also less likely to feel a mismatch in their fit to the organization, attenuating their intention to voluntarily leave the organization (Ibid).

Today, the focus on teamwork, empowerment, and flatter organizations puts a premium on organizational citizenship behavior that supports a membership that employees act instinctively to benefit both the organization and one's team. Fundamentally, employees who work as a team are more likely to feel an increased commitment to the work unit's efforts and the organization as a whole. Consequently, employees tend to remain in organizations due to the strong teamwork relationship they have established at the workplace (Clark 2001).

Satisfactory working environment

The factor most significantly affecting workforce commitment is management's recognition of the importance of personal and family life. For some employees, personal priorities or circumstances make the difference between leaving and staying. Individuals will stay with a company that clearly considers and cares for their career priorities (life stage needs), health, location, family, dual-career and other personal needs. For example, many companies are providing flexible schedules and work arrangements and are experimenting with other ways to help individuals manage their work and personal life issues (Solomon 1999).

Therefore, many companies have successfully created an employee-friendly environment by integrating specialized work arrangements such as flexible hours, telecommuting, and family-leave assistance to support employees in creating a work/life balance. Some researchers suggest that for positive work experiences to increase commitment significantly, employees must believe that such work experiences are a result of effective management policies. So parlaying a constructive culture into increased commitment might depend on how well managers succeed at getting employees to credit good management for their positive experiences (Parker and Wright 2001).

Impacts of Human Resource Management on Retention

Organizations develop human resource policies that genuinely reflect their beliefs and principles and the relationship between management and employees, or they may merely devise policies that deal with current problems or requirements. These practices include recruitment and selection, training and development, performance management, remuneration systems, occupational health and safety, industrial relations (Jackson and Schuler 1995).

Several theoreticians have argued that the human resources of the company are potentially the only source of sustainable competitive edge for organizations (Becker and Gerhart, 1996). Human resource system helps create a workforce whose contributions are valuable, unique, and difficult for competitors to imitate. Employees interpret organizational actions such as human resource practices and the trust worthiness of management. They reciprocate their perceptions accordingly in their own commitment to

34

the organization. A well-established stream of research rooted in social exchange theory has revealed that employees' commitment to the organization derives from their perceptions of the employers' commitment to and support of them (Ibid).

In this regard, a useful frame work in which to visualize commitment behavior is to View them as components of fair exchange between a company and its employees. This approach to motivation postulates that employees and the organizations are involved in an exchange relationship (Ibid). Employee attitudes and behaviors (including performance) reflect their perceptions and expectations, reciprocating the treatment that they receive from the organization.

Numerous studies suggest that high-involvement work practices will enhance employee retention. Most efforts on retention and commitment are considered from the employer's point of view. Flexible work schedules and childcare assistance was offered, but only a small share of the workforce takes advantage of them (Ibid). However, if the value proposition is viewed from the individual's perspective, different factors assume different weights. Baby boomers are more interested in job security and benefits; young employees are more interested in pay, advancement opportunities and time off. Such differences may reflect stages in the career cycle or deeper generation differences. Additionally, there are often gender differences within demographic groups; e.g., young women may want different things from what young men want (Noe 1999).

Over recent years, there has been a widespread assertion that HRM has become more strategic in its focus and operation (Fitz-enz 1990) . HRM is purportedly being viewed as a strategic staff enterprise aligned with organizational values, mission and vision. As a consequence, there is now much greater attention to measuring and enhancing employee and organizational performance; equal employment opportunity and affirmative action policies designed and implemented by personnel offices have contributed greatly to the diversity of the workforce; staffing techniques have become much more sophisticated; employee benefit systems have expanded; and job designs and processes have become more creative (Ibid).

Retention Management - A Strategic Tool

Researchers on retention have defined retention management as a strategic, coherent process that starts with an examination of the reasons that employees join an organization (Davies 2001), Studies have indicated that it is driven by several key factors, which should be managed congruently: organizational culture and structure, recruitment strategy, pay and benefits philosophy, employee support programs, and career development systems (Fitz-enz 1990). Careful career development and planning, as well as the more typical rewards and incentives, can be powerful retention tools. These should be effectively addressed as a corporate-wide initiative. Studies of progressive HRM practices in training, compensation and reward sharing have revealed that these can lead to reduced turnover and absenteeism, better quality work, and better financial performance (Delaney and Huselid 1996).

An employee's decision to resign from a company is rarely due to a single event, such as being passed over for a promotion, a plum assignment or for monetary reasons. One such event may however serve as a catalyst, but most employees leave because of multiple factors - the turnover drivers such' as diminished job satisfaction, a tense work environment and better advancement opportunities elsewhere (Davies 2001). Isolating these factors requires a disciplined research effort.

As turnover is a symptom of a larger systemic problem such as ineffective retention management, companies' ought to understand what causes people to commit themselves to being productive and loyal. Then they must design jobs, systems and organizations that support rather than inhibit it. Fostering commitment means an understanding that people need to have a stake in their work, and that employees respond when employers pay attention to their needs and involve them (Ibid).

To achieve quality retention programs, organizations ought to determine the retention factors relevant to each of their employee group, information can be gathered from current and former employees on their perceptions why people stay or leave. The more focused the analysis, the more focused the prescriptive actions may be. Providing a reasonably high level of attention to the factors important to employees will help for a strong organizational culture to be built and maintained (Ibid).

Several studies also suggest that high-involvement work practices will enhance employee retention (Arthur 1994). Various frameworks or models are used by organizations to address retention and commitment and some of the key factors are increasingly adopted and they include the following (Beck 2001):

Compensation: Companies often provide pay packages superior to the market for critical talent. These include special pay premiums, stock options or bonuses. Base pay reflects fair pay; supplemental programs reflect individual, team or organizational performance and success (Parker and Wright 2001).

Challenging work: High talent individuals want to work that is interesting, challenging and that has an impact on the company. They also expect work to be appropriately designed, with adequate resources available and with effective management. Increasingly, companies are redesigning work, relationships, workflows, and teams to create more exciting and challenging work (Beck 2001).

Work/relationships: Employees stay when they have strong relationships with others with whom they work (Clarke 2001). Companies encourage team building, project assignments involving work with peers and opportunities for social interaction both on and off the job (Arthur 1994). One value of team-based organizations is the bond that they establish among members and effective relationships with immediate managers are also important.

Recognition: Employees tend to stay when they feel that their capabilities, efforts, and performance contributions are recognized and appreciated by others. They want a sense of accomplishment. Compensation provides recognition, but other forms of non-monetary recognition are also important, for example from managers, team members and peers, customers, and others. Particularly important are opportunities to participate and to influence actions and decisions (Davies 2001).

Work/life balance: For some employees, personal priorities or circumstances make the difference between leaving and staying. Individuals will stay with a company that clearly considers and cares for their career priorities (life stage needs), health, location, family, dual-career and other personal needs (Arthur 1994).

Communication: Effective communications strengthen employee identification with the company and build trust. Increasingly, companies provide information on values, mission, strategies, competitive performance, and changes that may affect employees (Gorhart and Becker 2000). Many companies are working to provide information that employees want and need, through the most credible sources on a timely and consistent basis. Through such practices, companies are striving to improve employee retention.

Theoretical Frame work

A continuing organizational issue for manage merit and human resource personnel has been the retention of high performance employees. Researchers have suggested that reciprocity is a mechanism underlying commitment (Arthur 1994) and that employees will offer their commitment to the organization in reciprocation for the organization having fulfilled its psychological contract. By fulfilling obligations relating to, for example, pay, job security, and career development, employers are creating a need for employees to reciprocate, and this can take the form of attitudinal reciprocity through enhanced commitment (Arthur 1994).

In this project, turnover intention behavior (intent to stay) was selected as the focal dependent variable for the following reasons. First, employees purportedly view organizational commitment and turnover intention as acceptable commodities for exchange. Second, this variable has been demonstrated as salient with regard to a variety of exchange relationships (Shore and Wayne 1993).

The concept of commitment have established that employee commitment to the organization has a positive influence on job performance and a negative influence on intention to leave or employee turnover. Empirical evidence strongly supports the position that intent to stay or leave is strongly and consistently related to voluntary turnover (Arthur 1994).

The hypotheses formulated for the theoretical HRM-retention model of this study (Fig 1), conceptually considered the independent variables as "bundles" of HR practices (MacDuffie 1995). The independent variables consisted of eight factors grouped into two sets or bundles (i.e. HR factors and organizational factors). The decision to group them into bundles reinforced during the pre interview with general manager of the company.

Previous studies support the notion that practices within bundles are interrelated and the combined impact of practices in a bundle could be specified in two simple alternatives: an additive approach and a multiplicative approach. Statistically, the additive combination of practices has the desirable property that the sum of normally distributed variable scores is still normally distributed, which is not true for the multiplicative product. Conceptually, a multiplicative relationship implies that if any single organizational practice is not present, the "bundle" score (and effect) should be zero (Arthur 1994). However, Osterman (1994) argues that, "although practices in a bundle are expected to be interrelated, the absence of a particular practice will not: eradicate the effect of all other practices, but given the preceding arguments, this study has adopted the bundles of HR factors and organizational factors as complementary.

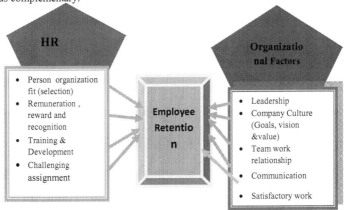

Figure 1 2: Model for the theoretical Frame work

39

Research Variables

The variables that are being considered are described in the theoretical framework. Employee retention is the dependent variable, which is going to be checked for a relationship with career development, supervisor support, working environment, rewards and work-life policies that are independent variables.

Independent Variables

①- Person- organization fit (Selection)

Person organization fit is considered a key part of organizational selection and is generally defined as "the compatibility between individuals and organizations" (Arthur 1994).

Person organization fit will be measured with a four items scale developed by Netemeyer et al. (1997). The measure reflects the fit between personal values and organizational values, for example "I feel that my personal values are a good fit with the organizational values." Employees prefer an ethical organizational environment. The fit between a company and its employees is strengthened when principled conduct is encouraged in organizations and this component of organizational value is also included in this measurement scale (Ibid).

②- Remuneration and recognition

Employees tend to remain with the organization when they feel their capabilities, efforts, and performance contributions are recognized and appreciated (Davies 2001). Remuneration and recognition will be measured with a five item scale focused on intrinsic and extrinsic rewards. Extrinsic reward measures were designed to measure the employee's view of the economic rewards from his/her job. It includes pay, benefits, and job security. The scale also measured the degree to which intrinsic rewards such as recognition are present in the organization (Ibid).

③ - Training 'and Career Development

Training provides employees with specific skills or helps to correct deficiencies in their performance; while development is an effort to provide employees with abilities the organization will need in the future (Arthur 1994).

A four item scale developed by focused on whether the organization expends sufficient effort in providing opportunities for people to develop their skills, and the adequacy of the training (Ibid).

④- Challenging assignments

Providing employees with challenging assignments with well-defined performance measures and feedback is important for a high performance environment in which employees can achieve their personal a objectives (Jackson, et al 1993).

A five item scale will derived from the Job Diagnostic Survey to measure challenging assignments. The scale explored job elements of skill variety, task significance, task identity, autonomy, high order needs and feedback (Ibid).

⑤-Leadership Behavior

Research findings suggest that leadership enhances organizational commitment. Positive influence of transformation leaders on organizational outcomes, resulting in lowered intention to leave and increased organizational citizenship behavior.

A four items scale will measure leadership behavior. The scale consisted of items adapted from two validated scales: (1) the Multifactor Leadership Questionnaire devised by Bass and Avolio (1990), which measured transformational leadership and (2) the eight-item. The adapted scale used in this study measured leadership behavior in terms of leadership effectiveness, extra effort and leadership satisfaction (Podsekoff et al 1996).

⑥ -Team work relationship

41

Employees stay when they have' strong relationships with others they work with (Clarke 2001). Team building, assignments involving work with peers, and opportunities for social interaction both on and off the job encourage these relationships (Ibid).

A four item scale developed by Bass and Avolio (1990) will measure the team leadership and relationship of employees and peer leadership, in this study.

⑦ - Organizational culture and policies

Company culture is described as the invisible forces that shape life in a business organization (Fitz-enz 1990). Management philosophy and style, communications protocol and policies, rituals and taboos all interact to create the uniqueness of each company culture.

A five item scale modified from The Organization Profile Questionnaire (Podsekoff et al 1996) developed by was used to measure organizational culture. The profile is a descriptive instrument, one that paints a picture of respondents' views of their organization's culture. The scale measures the degree the organizational structure limits the action of employees, the focus on the influence of policies and procedures, and tests organizational goal clarity and planning.

⑧ -Work environment

Many companies are providing flexible schedules and work arrangements and are experimenting with other ways to help individuals manage their work and personal life issues. Individuals will stay with a company that clearly considers and cares for their career priorities (life stage needs), health, location, family, dual-career, and other personal needs (Shepherd and Mathews 2000).

A seven-item scale derived from several scales will design to measure humanistic and socialization, physical work conditions and organizational climate. Three items will measure the extent to which the individual is respected and cared for by the organization. Three items will measure perceptions about the organizational climate in the workplace. One item will measure the physical conditions experienced in the workplace (Ibid)

Dependent Variables

◆ *Organizational Commitment*

Organizational commitment consists of three components: '(1) identification, pride in the organization and the internalization of its goals and values; (2) involvement – psychological absorption in the activities of one's role for the good of the employing organization; and (3) loyalty – affection for, and attachment to the organization' (Shepherd and Mathews 2000).

Organizational commitment was measured using nine items from the fifteen item Organizational Commitment Questionnaire (OCQ) scale developed by (Mowday et al, 1979).

◆ *Turn over intention (Intent to Stay) [*

According to (Mowday et al, 1979), "the best single predictor of an individual's behavior will be a measure of the intention to perform that behavior". Empirical evidence strongly supports the position that intent to stay or leave is strongly and consistently related to voluntary turnover (Ibid).

Intent to stay (Turnover intention) was measured with a four-item scale consisting of items adapted from the Michigan Organizational Assessment Questionnaire. Using a five-point scale, respondents will rate the likelihood of staying at the job; whether they thought about quitting; their degree of loyalty and the likelihood of looking for a new job in the near future.

Hypothesis

Based on the above conceptual model the following hypothesis (H) has been formulated for this study.

Human resource Factor Bundle

H1: Person- organization fit (Selection) positively influence intention of stay

H2: Remuneration recognition and reward positively influence intention of stay

H3: Opportunities for Training 'and Career Development positively influences intention of stay

H4: Challenging employment assignments and opportunities positively influence intention of stay

Organizational factor Bundle

H5: Strong Leadership direction and coordination positively influence intention of stay
H6: Organizational culture and policies positively influence intention of stay

H7: Team work relationship positively influence intention of stay

H8: satisfactory Work environment positively influence intention of stay

H9: Both Human resource Factor Bundle and Organizational factor Bundle have not equally positively influence for intention to stay

H10: Organizational commitment impacts upon the relationships between the:

(a) HR factor bundle and intent to stay, and

(b) Organizational factor bundle and intent to stay.

Chapter Four

Discussion and Analysis

Dashen Brewery was established at the historical town of Gondar-Ethiopia with an initial investment capital of over birr 340 million. It is named after mount Dashen, Ethiopia's highest mountain (elevation 4,523 meters). Dashen Brewery produces two types of product namely bottled and draught beer and started to supply its product June 2000; The Brewery had production capacity of 300,000 HL per annum which was expanded to 750,000HL per annum with additional investment cost of birr 110 million. It covers an area of 85,000sq.meter with building area of 12,000sq.meter. The company has 490 permanent and contract employees excluding induced labors/locals.

Figure 2. Dashen Brewery factory

The company operates in line of the following vision and mission statements.

Vision

- Make Dashen the central venue for quality beer celebrities.

Mission

- Producing and selling customer proffered quality beer at competitive price and generate reasonable profit.

Note: The organizational structure of Dashen Brewery annexed at appendix C

This chapter reports the results of the study and it include the following: demographic profiles, means, and standard deviations, the results of the factor analysis and correlation analysis, and the outcomes of the regression tests. For this study, the sample was severely skewed and therefore data transformation occurred.

Demographic Profile

Table 2 presents the demographic data of the respondents depicting the proportion of sex, age, qualification, Department, and experience of the participants of the project.

Table 2: demographic characteristics of respondents

Sex	Frequency (N=74)	Percent (100%)
Female	9	12.9
Male	65	87.1
Qualification		
Diploma	38	50.5
First degree	36	49.5
Experience (in years):		
0-2	27	36.6
3-5	23	30.9
6-10	13	17.5
above 10 years	11	14.9

A total of seventy five questionnaires were distributed for employees working in eight deferent departments of the factory. Ninety percent (n=74) of these employees responded, of which eight seven percent were male and thirteen percent were female.

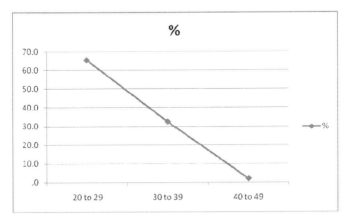

Figure 3: Age of respondents

The age of the respondents, were identified in three specific categories; 65.5 percent were aged between twenty and twenty-nine; 32.5 percent between thirty and thirty-nine; 2 percent between forty and forty-nine.

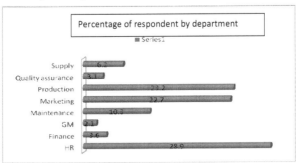

Figure 4: Respondents by Departments

The respondents of this study consisted of all permanent employees from eight departments of Dashen Brewery. 28.9 percent of these respondents were from Human Resource department, 22.7 percent from marketing, 6.2 percent from supplies, 3.1 percent from quality assurance, 3.6 percent from finance, 23.2 percent from production, 10.3percent from maintenance, and 2.1percent from general manager staffs.

As shown in Table 2, the qualification of the respondents consisted of 50.5 percent diploma graduates and 49.5 percent degree holders. The service year of the respondents identified four categories; 36.6 percent of the respondents between 0-2 years of experience, 30.9 percent in between 3-5 years of experience, 17 percents were between 6-10 years, and 14.9 percents of the participants were above 10 years of experience. This study includes a good range of employment services and therefore provided a much broader scope for generating the research.

Exploratory Factor Analysis

The nine independent variables (1) person organization fit, 2) remuneration and recognition, 3) training and career development, 4) challenging assignments, 5) leadership behavior, 6) communication and consultation, 7) teamwork relationship, 8) company culture and policies, and 9) work environment were factor analyzed (principal components with varimax rotation). The goal of varimax rotation is to simplify factors by maximizing the variance of the loadings within factors, across variables. The spread in loadings is maximized; loadings that are high after extraction become higher after rotation and loadings that are low become lower. Consequently, interpreting a factor becomes easier because it is obvious which variables correlate (Neter, Kutner, Nachtsheim and Wasserman 1996).

Table 3: Factor analysis of the variable items

Rotated Component Matrix[a]

Variables	Items	Loading Scores
Person Organization fit	This organization has the same values as I do with regard to concern for others.	.098
	This organization does not have the same value as I do with regard to fairness.	.648
	This organization has the same values as I do with regard to honesty.	.703
	I feel that my personal values are a good fit with this organizational culture.	.825
Reward and Recognition	Employees are given positive recognition when they produce high quality work	-.116
	This organization pays well.	.922
	This organization offers a good benefits package compared to other organizations.	.936
	This organization values individual excellence over teamwork.	.398
	This organization offers good opportunities for Promotion.	.152

48

Training & Career Development	People are properly orientated and trained upon joining this organization.	.689
	This organization does provide opportunities for personal & career development	.790
	Innovation and creativity are encouraged here.	.859
	The organization has career development activities to help an employees	.790
Challenging Assign,& opportunities	Employees are offered more challenging work within the organization.	.226
	Employees can work autonomously on their work assignments.	.871
	Employees are skilled to do a number of different jobs, not just one particular job.	.751
	Employees are given opportunities to learn new things.	.422
	Employees are offered a good amount of variety in their job.	.814
Organizational Leadership	The leadership practices help me to become a high performing employee.	.947
	The leadership practices in this organization enhance my satisfaction with my job.	.960
	The organizational leadership practices are consistent with my personal values.	.767
	The organizational leadership practices make a positive contribution to the overall effectiveness of the organization.	.910
Team Relationship	Team working is valued in this organization.	.874
	Members of my team expect and maintain high standards of performance.	.715
	Team leaders are recognized for promotion and development.	.000
	Each member of my team has a clear idea of the group's goals.	.645
Organizational policies	Organizational policies and procedures are helpful, well understood and up to date.	.806
	Progress towards meeting planned objectives is periodically reviewed.	.770
	The organizational structure facilitates the way we do things.	.703
	This organization has a defined vision/mission to meet its goals.	.465
Communication	This organization keeps employees well- informed on matters important to them.	.843
	Sufficient effort is made to determine the thoughts and responses of employees	.828
	Communications across all levels in this organization tend to be good	.847
	Organizational structure encourages horizontal and vertical communication.	.598
	There is trust between employees and their supervisors/team leaders.	.646
Working Environment	My working life balances with my family life.	.715
	Overall this organization is a harmonious place to work.	.365
	This organization regards welfare of its employees as its first priority.	.714
	Workers and management get along in this Organization.	.833
	For the work I do, the physical working conditions are very pleasant	.180
	This organization offers a lot of security.	-.152
	A spirit of cooperation and teamwork exists.	.518
Organizational Commitment	I feel a strong sense of belonging to this company.	-.672
	I could just as well be working for a different company if the type of work was similar.	.085
		.763
	Often I find it difficult to agree with this company's policies on important matters relating to its employees.	.165
	This company really inspires the very best in me in the way of job performance.	-.094
	I find that my values and this company's values are very similar	.594
	There is little to be gained by sticking with this Company indefinitely	-.552
	I am willing to put in a great deal more effort than normally expected to help this company be successful.	-.022
	I am proud to tell others that I am part of this company	-.186
	I really care about the fate of this company	
Turn over Imitation (intent to stay)	I plan to work at my present job for as long as possible	.847
	I will most certainly look for a new job in the near future	-.813
	I plan to stay in this job for at least two to three years.	.719
	I would hate to quit this job	-.002

Extraction Method: Principal Component Analysis.   Rotation Method: Varimax with Kaiser Normalization.

a.   Rotation converged in 3 iterations.

The correlation of the factors is ascertained from the pattern matrix displayed in Table 3. The results support the factorial independence of eight of the nine constructs. The two dependent variables, organizational commitment and intention to stay (turnover intention), were also factor analyzed (varimax rotation) in a separate analysis.

As a result of the exploratory factor analysis several items (i.e. items which are marked by bold) were deleted from the variables, due to cross loadings. Items which has lees cross loading Cross loading score of <0.30 were deleted, as they were not considered to be adding to the measure, reducing the items of dependent and independent variables.

The resultant items under the factors included person organization fit (items reduced from four to three), remuneration and recognition(items reduced from five to three), training and career development(all the four items are retained), challenging assignments(items reduced from five to four),organizational leadership behavior (all the four items are retained), teamwork relationship(all the four items are retained), company culture and policies(all the four items are retained), communication(all the five items are retained), work environment(items reduced from seven to five), organizational commitment(items reduced from nine to six), and intention to stay(items reduced from four to three).items that are deleted from each variable will be removed from further analysis.

4.3. Means, Mode and Standard deviations

Independent variables

1. HR factor bundles

Table 4: Mean, Mode and standard deviation of Human resource factors

Person -Organization Fit	Descriptive values					
Items	N	Mean	Mode	Std. Deviation	Mini	Max
This organization does not have the same value as I do with regard to fairness.	194	3.54	4	0.86	2	5
This organization has the same values as I do with regard to honesty.	194	3.49	4	0.93	2	5
I feel that my personal values are a good fit with this organizational culture.	194	3.78	5	1.02	2	5
Reward and Recognition						
This organization pays well.	194	3.24	4	1.27	1	5
This organization offers a good benefits package compared to other organizations.	194	3.27	4	1.18	1	5
This organization values individual excellence over teamwork.	194	2.82	4	1.13	1	5
Training and Development						
People are properly orientated and trained upon joining this organization.	194	3.165	4	1.17	1	5
This organization does provide regular opportunities for personal and career development	194	2.78	3	1.17	1	5
Innovation and creativity are encouraged here.	194	2.68	3	1.15	1	5
The organization has career development activities	194	2.82	3	1.26	1	5
Challenging Employment Assignment and Opportunities						
Employees can work autonomously on their work assignments.	194	3.51	4	1.21	1	5
Employees are skilled to do a number of different jobs, not just one particular job.	194	3.12	4	1.26	1	5
Employees are given opportunities to learn new things.	194	2.47	1	1.27	1	5

The above table enumerates the mean, mode and standard deviation of items under human resource factor bundles. If the selection process is deficient, it can lead to employees leaving earlier than their employer would like them to, thus increasing turnover costs. It could also allow poor performers enter and stay in the organization, driving down its performance. In the case of Dashen Brewery the mean of the items shows that most of the participants were agreed on their personal value regarding fairness and honesty were properly aligned the victory values and culture. This was further supported by the mode value of each item.

51

In responding to their satisfaction with the rewards and recognition they receive, the participants responded that on average their satisfaction is between neutral and satisfied. The mean score, as shown on the table, was 3.24 and 3.27 with three being neutral and four being satisfied. The range for the responses was one to five with one representing strongly disagree and five representing strongly agree on the items of reward and recognition factor. Even though the mean and mode value of the items under reward and recognition naked that most of the respondents are fall on the right side of the midpoint (3); significant portion of the participants were not agree on the reward and recognition given by the company. To solve such problems it is advisable to use pay-for-knowledge/contribution system.

The system provides Dashen Brewery with at least three key advantages. First the enhanced flexibility of its core cross-trained workforce means that the company can effectively manage the demands of seasonal business peaks when less experienced contract group is brought in. Second, employees who receive a pay premium for their knowledge/contribution are less likely to move to other competing companies with more traditional job-based pay systems. Third, it has increased morale, with employees self-motivated to increase skill levels and commitments.

Three items of the training and development variable were scored a mean value of less than three; this shows that the company did not provide regular opportunities for personal and career developments; innovation and creativity were not encouraged; and also the factory were not have career development plans. In any event, retention reflects a desire to keep one's valued people; but it is just as much about keeping and managing the skills that a company needs to meet its goals. The provision of training is a way of developing those skills in the first place. The fact that providing it also turns out to be a benefit that is highly valued by those who receive it makes for a very powerful approach to doing business. Countless studies tend to confirm the fact that a good part of the satisfaction or dissatisfaction of workers is associated with issues related to their professional development.

Thus, one of the basic elements for employee productivity and retention were not properly implemented. This may be one possible cause for employee decision for not to stay in the factory. Investing in training can be interpreted as a strong signal that the employer values the employee and wishes to keep that individual with the firm. To the extent that employees perceive this to be the case, and provided that the way the company actually behaves in such a way by 'putting its money where its mouth is' employees may in fact be more likely to stay. The training incentive is further reinforced if it falls within well-defined and adequately communicated plans for professional development within the company. Therefore the training and career development programs in the factory need to be revised.

Similarly the mean and mode value of the item shows there is no opportunities to learn new things for employees. In any event, if one company needs to promote good retention strategy; it should allow greater autonomy on the job, presenting more interesting challenges, or increasing the diversity of tasks by means of creating new opportunities for learning.

2. Organizational Factor Bundle

Table 5: Mean, Mode and standard deviation of Organizational factors

Organizational Leadership	Descriptive values					
Items	N	Mean	Mode	Std. Deviation	Mini	Max
The leadership practices in this organization help me to become a high performing employee.	194	2.78	4	1.21	1	5
The leadership practices in this organization enhance my satisfaction with my job.	194	2.85	3	1.29	1	5
The organizational leadership practices are consistent with my personal values.	194	2.72	2	1.08	1	5
The organizational leadership practices make a positive contribution to the overall effectiveness of the organization.	194	2.87	2	1.47	1	5
Team Relationship						
Team working is valued in this organization.	194	3.43	4	1.38	1	5
Members of my team expect and maintain high standards of performance.	194	3.58	4	1.10	1	5
Each member of my team has a clear idea of the group's goals.	194	3.74	4	0.96	1	5
Organizational Policies						

53

Organizational policies and procedures are helpful, well understood and up to date.	194	3.81	4	0.97	1	5
Progress towards meeting planned objectives is periodically reviewed.	194	3.33	4	1.17	1	5
The organizational structure facilitates the way we do things.	194	3.66	4	1.14	1	5
This organization has a defined vision/mission to meet its goals.	194	3.93	4	1.06	1	5
Communication					
This organization keeps employees well- informed on matters important to them.	194	3.03	4	1.198	1	5
Sufficient effort is made to determine the thoughts and responses of people who work here.	194	2.86	4	1.089	1	5
Communications across all levels in this organization tend to be good	194	2.98	4	1.386	1	5
Organizational structure encourages horizontal and vertical communication.	194	3.34	4	1.432	1	5
There is trust between employees and their supervisors/team leaders.	194	3.25	4	1.327	1	5
Working Environment					
My working life balances with my family life.	194	2.85	4	1.325	1	5
Overall this organization is a harmonious place to work.	194	3.21	3	1.186	1	5
This organization regards welfare of its employees as its first priority.	194	2.78	4	1.155	1	5
Workers and management get along in this Organization.	194	4.26	4	6.681	1	4
A spirit of cooperation and teamwork exists.	194	3.52	4	1.197	1	5

The average numbers of the respondents neither agree nor disagree on that the organization's leadership practices help them to become a high performing employee but those who respond 'agree' was greater in number and for most of them the leadership practices in the organization neither did not enhance nor did enhance their satisfaction with their job even the organizational leadership practices are not consistent with their personal values for most of the respondents. Again the average and greater number of the respondents did not believe that the organizational leadership practices make a positive contribution to the overall effectiveness of the organization. So the organizational leadership quality is questionable as indicated in the table above.

Significant number of respondents believed that work place team relationship was somewhat valued at the factory; the mean of the respondents for the variable is in between neutral and agree. The overall descriptive value of communication explicitly shows that communication across departments and two-way feedback was weak .Open, responsive, two-way communications would appear to be vital to good employee retention. The rationale for good communications is best summed up by Kaye and Jordan-Evans (1999).

Conspicuously withholding information can lead to deleterious consequences within the organization. When top leaders share information and expect other managers to share it with employees, employees tend to feel more included and their trust is reinforced, resulting in smaller dips in productivity during crises. Additionally, informed employees are sometimes able to provide solutions to otherwise unresolved problems. Information sharing includes: strategic directions, the organization's and industry's future, emerging trends that could affect career possibilities, and other cultural political realities affecting the organization. These types of information help to support employee career development and advancement.

It's very important to recognize the emerging needs of individuals to keep them committed and provide the work environment as necessitate (Ramlall, 2003). Milory (2004) reported that people enjoy working, and strive to work in those organizations that provide positive work environment where they feel they are making difference and where most people in the organization are proficient and pulling together to move the organization forward. Considerable numbers of respondents were disagreed on their working life balances with their family life and the company's practice regards welfare. The responses of participants' ranges from strongly disagree to strongly agree for all items under the variable working environment. As I demonstrated the physical/work environment of the company; contributes as a major factor effecting the decision of employee's whether to stay.

4.4. Correlation analysis

Table 6: Pearson Correlation results between independent and the dependent variable

HR-Bundles	Correlation Values	Organizational Commitment	Intention to stay
Person -organization fit	Pearson Correlation	.186**	.239**
	Sig. (1-tailed)	.010	.001
Remuneration and recognition	Pearson Correlation	.222**	.351**
	Sig. (1-tailed)	.002	.000

Training and career development	Pearson Correlation	.209**	.371**
	Sig. (1-tailed)	.003	.000
Challenging assignments	Pearson Correlation	.171*	.219**
	Sig. (1-tailed)	.017	.002
Organizational -bundles			
Leadership behavior	Pearson Correlation	.265**	.515**
	Sig. (1-tailed)	.000	.000
Teamwork relationship	Pearson Correlation	.233**	.016
	Sig. (1-tailed)	.001	.825
Organizational policies	Pearson Correlation	.444**	.224**
	Sig. (1-tailed)	.000	.002
Communication	Pearson Correlation	.316**	.298**
	Sig. (1-tailed)	.000	.000
Work environment	Pearson Correlation	.136	.503**
	Sig. (1-tailed)	.059	.000

The correlation matrix presented in Table 6 revealed that all the nine variables (person organization-fit, remuneration and recognition, training and career development, challenging assignments, and leadership behavior, teamwork relationship, culture and policies, communication and work environment) have significant positive correlations with a) organizational commitment and b) intention to stay. The direction of the association ranged from r= 0.016 to r=0.515. These results indicate no multi-co linearity and singularity problems. The correlation results meant that H1, H2, H3, H4, H5, H6, H7, H8, H9 were supported.

Person organization, remuneration and recognition, training and career development, challenging assignments of the human resource factors bundle were to be found critical and significant for employees' decision ether to leave or stay. More over these factors were significantly correlated with organizational commitment of employees. In addition to human resource factors; leadership behavior culture and policies, communication and work environment were significant for retention of employees. Team work relationship has weak significance over intention to stay. Therefore, the effectiveness of employee retention strategy and management of Dashen Brewery highly depends on the trends and practices the above factors(person organization-fit-r=.239** , remuneration and recognition-r=.351**, training and career development-r=.371**, challenging assignments-r=.219**, and leadership behavior-r=.515**, culture and policies-r=.224**, communication-r= .298**,and work environment bundle-r=.503**; p<0.05).

Table 7: Pearson Correlation results between demographic factors and the dependent variable

Variables	Correlation Values	Demographic factors				
		Sex	Age	Qualification	Department	Experience (in years):
Organizational Commitment	Pearson Correlation	-.122	.116	.002	-.020	.087
	Sig. (2-tailed)	.090	.106	.974	.778	.226
Turn over intention	Pearson Correlation	.085	-.025	.076	-.055	-.061
	Sig. (2-tailed)	.239	.734	.293	.448	.397

The demographic variables showed only weak associations with the commitment dimension and intention to stay. Both age (r= .116, p<0.05) and sex (r = -.122, p<0.05) were positively and negatively correlated to organizational commitment respectively but qualification, department, and experience had no significant relationship. Even though there level of significant were near zero; sex and qualification were positively correlate with intention to stay and age, department, and experience were negatively correlated. Therefore qualification, department, and experience were removed from further analyses in the interests of parsimony.

Table 8: Pearson Correlation results among dependent variable

Dependent Variables	Correlation Values	Organizational Commitment	Intention to stay
Organizational Commitment	Pearson Correlation	1	.246**
	Sig. (1-tailed)		.001
Intention to stay	Pearson Correlation	.246**	1
	Sig. (1-tailed)	.001	

The association between organizational commitment and intention to stay (r =.246, p<0.001) was strong, positive, and significant. Thus, as the correlation analysis indicated; there are significant relationships between the identified factors and organizational commitment and intent to stay. However under the organizational factor bundle work place team relationship and working environment were not significant turnover intention and organizational commitment.

Multiple Regressions

In this study, a stepwise multiple regression process was used to examine the relationships between eight HRM factors, organizational commitment and intent to stay. In addition, age and gender were used as control variables in the regression analysis. The regression analyses ran with two separate sets of independent variables (HR factors and organizational factors). The reason for this is conceptually based. In this study, the choices about bundling HR practices began with the design of the theoretical model. The independent variables were divided into two bundles (HR factors and Organizational factors) identified from the theoretical frame work of the project.

Each of these bundles is made up of interrelated, internally consistent and even overlapping practices. The two bundles are complementary. It is the combination of practices in a bundle, rather than individual practices that shapes the pattern of interactions between the employers and employees (Tabachnik and Fidell 2001). Statistically it also makes sense to separate out these bundles to show the true effect. Regression is best when each IV is strongly related to the DV but uncorrelated to other variables (Ibid). Thus the regression solution is extremely sensitive to the combination of variables that is included in it. Whether or not independent variables (IVs) appear particularly important in a solution depends upon the other IVs in the set. Clearly, there were strong correlations between the HRM factors.

As such, two separate regression equations were developed and tested in this study. The regression equations tested were of the following form:

Equation 1: HR Factors bundle + commitment + constant = Turnover intention (intent to stay)

And

Equation 2: Organizational Factors + commitment + constant = Turnover intention (intent to stay).

58

Table 9: Regression Results (Unstandardised Coefficients) for Organizational Commitment as Dependent Variable

Dependent variable: Organizational Commitment		Coefficients[a]				
Model	Predictors	Unstandardized Coefficients		Standardized Coefficients		
		B	Std. Error	Beta	t	Sig.
1	(Constant)	2.840	.223		12.759	.000
	Person organizational fit	.100	.056	.130	1.778	.077
	Reward and recognition	.057	.056	.105	1.019	.310
	Training and development	.038	.049	.081	.775	.439
	Challenging assg.& opp.	.054	.044	.093	1.224	.222
Model summary	R					.283[a]
	R²					.080
	Adjusted R²					.061
	Std. Error of the Estimate					.426
Model	Predictors	Unstandardized Coefficients		Standardized Coefficients	t	Sig.
		B	Std. Error	Beta		
1	(Constant)	2.494	.193		12.923	.000
	Organizational leadership	-.040	.048	-.104	-.842	.401
	Team relationship	.070	.045	.126	1.566	.119
	Organizational Policy	.213	.052	.364	4.073	.000
	Communication	.058	.046	.128	1.281	.202
	Working Environment	.021	.035	.059	.607	.545
	R					.461[a]
	R²					.212
	Adjusted R²					.192
	Std. Error of the Estimate					.395

As shown in the table 9, human resource factor bundle have positive relationship with organizational commitment. However, none of the variables under the HR factor bundle were not found as significant for organizational commitment ($p < 0.05$). This result discovered that person organizational fit, reward and recognition as well as training and development practices under the current circumstances of the factory were not significantly support organizational commitment. Among the variables of Human Resource factor bundle; person organization fit relatively in a better way; it has greater coefficient(R) compare to other factors under the bundle.

Person organization, reward and recognition, training and development, challenging assignment, and opportunities account 6.1 percent of the variance in commitment. This shows that, the human resource factor bundle has low level of significance for organizational commitment currently. Organizational policy significantly influence organizational commitment (B=0.213, p< 0.05) and organizational leadership negatively influence employee commitment at Dashen Brewery.   Team relationship, Communication, and Working Environment were found insignificant for commitment. Organizational factor bundle contribute 19.20% for commitment. All in all the result illustrate that organizational factor bundle better than human resource factor bundle for the commitment of employees in Dashen brewery.

Table 10: Regression Results (Unstandardised Coefficients) for Intention to stay as Dependent Variable

Dependent Variable: Turnover Intention		**Coefficients**[a]				
Model	Predictors	Unstandardized Coefficients		Standardized Coefficients	t	Sig.
		B	Std. Error	Beta		
1	(Constant)	1.903	.249		7.644	.000
	Person organizational fit	.145	.063	.159	2.302	.022
	Reward and recognition	.079	.062	.122	1.257	.210
	Training and development	.131	.055	.233	2.373	.019
	Challenging assg.& oppo.	.052	.049	.075	1.052	.294
	R					.429[a]
	R^2					.189
	Adjusted R^2					.166
	Std. Error of the Estimate					.476

The result revealed that, the study hypotheses (H1, H2, H3 and H4) that predicted person organization fit, remuneration, recognition and reward and challenging opportunities positively influence intention to stay are supported by the data. Person organization fit, and training and development were significant (B=0.145 & 0.131 respectively p<0.05) for intention to stay. Human resource factor bundle account 16.6 percent of the variance in intention to stay. The beta value 0.079 demonstrate that the impact of reward and recognition that practiced by the company was poor. The more frequently the employee sees thinks about, or uses the reward, the more the employee is expected to realize that he/she is valued by the organization; thereby it increased the level of employee Retention. From the theoretical frame work and related literature, the result reveals that improving the rewards and recognition scheme will results into higher employee retention in the company.

Table 11: Regression Results (Unstandardised Coefficients) for Intention to stay as Dependent Variable

Dependent Variable: Turn over intention		Coefficients[a]				
		Unstandardized Coefficients		Standardized Coefficients		
Model	Predictors	B	Std. Error	Beta	t	Sig.
1	(Constant)	2.792	.188		14.877	.000
	Organizational leadership	.182	.046	.396	3.918	.000
	Team relationship	-.231	.043	- .352	-5.320	.000
	Organizational Policy	-.125	.051	-.180	-2.456	.015
	Communication	.163	.044	.301	3.667	.000
	Working Environment	.189	.034	.444	5.533	.000
	R	.686[a]				
	R^2	.471				
	Adjusted R^2	.475				
	Std. Error of the Estimate	.384				

The results of the stepwise multiple regression analysis indicated that team relation had the highest beta value contributed 23.1% to the variance in turn over intention. Organizational leadership and working environment contributed about 18.2% and 16.3% respectively. Organizational culture and policy contributed 12.5% variation for intention to stay.

Organizational factors of leadership, communication, and work environment, have a strong and positive influence on employees' intention to stay. The result supports H5 (strong leadership direction and coordination positively influence intention of stay), and H8 (working environment). On the other hand teamwork relationship and company policies have strong negative influence; accordingly H6 (organizational policies positively influence intention to stay), and H7 (team work relationship positively influence intention to stay) were rejected by the data. However, organizational factor bundle accounting for 47.1% of the variance in intention to stay.

The result reveals that organizational leadership, team relation, organizational policy, communication and working environment were major independent variable that significantly affect and contribute for employee retention management practices of Dashen Brewery. Amongst all the determinants; team relationship, as it has the highest beta value which is 0.231, this shows a very significant relationship with the employee retention which means if employees are endowed with more work place team relationship then the employee retention will be increased to a great deal. The beta value of work environment is 0.189 which shows a very significant relationship with the employee intention to stay means if employees are working in a very good environment then it will add considerable positive impact on employee retention. So the research result reveals that the affect of work environment on employees is very much. It leads to feel employees happy and keep active to perform various job tasks. It is important to note that organizations exist in environments, in which they have been operated. Work environment influences especially when one considers employee retention.

The beta value of work-life policies is 0.125 which exhibit that work- life policies have an impact on Employee Retention. It is the most recent addition to the research in the employee retention and plays a role of obtaining a balance between work and life. It encourages employee's decision to remain with the organization. It has been evident that when employees of the company have been provided a balance in their work and family life, they showed more loyalty and a greater level of retention in the organization. Its concurrence can cause an intention to stay in the organization as well as solve the issues between family members and family activities.

Similarly, organizational leadership, organizational policy, communication, and working environment significantly influence turn over intention. Forming and implementing proper organizational leadership, team relationship, organizational policy, communication and working environment results into higher employee retention. Organizational factor bundle is the most influential variable in deciding the employee retention.47.5% of the variance for employee intention to stay accounted by organizational factors.

The results of this study have clearly shown that the independent variables which are Organizational leadership, organizational policy, team relationship, Communication, and working environment have a direct impact on the dependent variable that is employee retention which means the enhancement of one independent variable causes the enhancement in the employee retention which is the dependent variable. Today it has become crucial to have a committed, loyal and retained work force, as it is the one whose loyalty can actually pay off in the long run to gain a competitive edge in the business. Therefore if the Dashen Brewery work on these determinants and apply them in the organization it would definitely foster the employee retention.

Table 12: Regression Results (Unstandardised Coefficients) for Turnover Intention with the mediation of commitment

Dependent Variable: Turn over intention		Coefficients[a]				
		Unstandardized Coefficients		Standardized Coefficients		
Model –	HR factors	B	Std. Error	Beta	t	Sig.
1	(Constant)	1.433	.337		4.254	.000
	Person organizational fit	.128	.063	.141	2.039	.043
	Reward and recognition	.069	.062	.107	1.113	.267
	Training and development	.125	.055	.222	2.274	.024
	Challenging assg.& oppo.	.043	.049	.062	.874	.383
	Orag_commitement	.166	.081	.139	2.053	.041
Model summary	R	.449[a]				
	R Square	.202				
	Adjusted R Square	.180				
	Std. Error of the Estimate	.47239				

Baron and Kenny (1986) highlight that a variable is considered mediator if: (a) the 1 predictor variable are significantly correlated with the hypothesis mediator,(b) the predictor and mediator variables are all significantly correlated with the dependent variable, and (c) a previously significant effect for the predictor variables when the dependent variable is regressed into them, becomes non-significant or significantly reduced in predicting power when the hypothesized mediator is added to the analysis.

The table reports the results of Equation (1) regression analysis testing for the indirect effect of commitment on intention to stay when the independent variables are the HR bundle. The results from table 12 suggest that commitment plays a differential role in affecting the relationship between HR factors and intent to stay. For instance, the results suggest that commitment completely mediates the relationship between the factors of reward and recognition, and challenging opportunity and intention to stay; whilst only partially mediating the relationship between person organization fit, training and development and intent to stay. The regression result shows commitment has significant impact on the relationship of human resource factor bundle and intention to stay. With the mediation of commitment, Person organizational fit, and training and development were significant for turn over intention and as a sum human resource factor contribute 18% of the variance for intention to stay.

Table 13 : Regression Results (Unstandardised Coefficients) for Turnover Intention as Dependent Variable with the mediation of commitment

Dependent Variable: Turnover intention		Coefficients[a]				
		Unstandardized Coefficients		Standardized Coefficients		
Model	Predictors –Organ factor	B	Std. Error	Beta	t	Sig.
1	(Constant)	2.236	.252		8.882	.000
	Organizational leadership	.191	.045	.416	4.205	.000
	Team relationship	-.246	.043	-.376	-5.782	.000
	Organizational Policy	-.173	.052	-.248	-3.330	.001
	Communication	.150	.043	.277	3.441	.001
	Working Environment	.184	.033	.433	5.521	.000
	Organizational commitment	.223	.069	.188	3.223	.001
model Summary	R	.449[a]				
	R Square	.202				
	Adjusted R Square	.180				
	Std. Error of the Estimate	.47239				

Research has shown that employees' commitment to an organization affects how well the organization performs in various ways. If it turns out that employee commitment varies in certain predictable ways from one cultural pattern to another, organizational development specialists could try to strengthen employee commitment and, therefore, organizational effectiveness by changing the organizational culture. Table 13 specifically reveals that commitment mediates the relationship between teamwork, culture and intent to stay and acts as a possible partial mediator of the relationship between work environment and intent to stay.

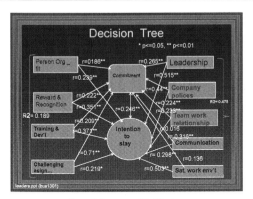

Figure 5 **Summary of Decision tree**

Results revealed that organizational commitment mediates teamwork relationships and organizational culture and policies and act as a partial mediator of work environment. Commitment has a strong impact on the relationship between organizational factor bundle and intent to stay. Equation 2 has tested based on the regression result on table 13. With the intervention of commitment, organizational factor account 18% of the variance for intention to stay. All the variables under the organizational factor bundle were significantly affect intention to stay. Both team relationship and organizational Policy negatively influence intention to stay with and without the mediation of commitment.

Summary of the Focus Group Discussion (FGD)

A total of 12 participants were parts of the focus group discussion (FGD). The members were from top and middle level management, labour union, and employees (see the picture below). The discussions were carried for two hours and different questions were adequately discussed by the participants and the following points were summarized and presented as follows.

| Ato Solomon Alebel | Getie Andualem(PhD) | Birhanu G | Ato Mekibib Alemu |
| Assistant | Modulator | Researcher | General Manager |

Department Managers, labour union leaders and employee employees

Figure 6: Pictures of FGD participants and facilitators

The participants were asked whether the company adopt one standardized human resource practice for every employee within the firm (a holistic approach) or apply differential HR practices for different types of employees. Accordingly, all most all participants of FGD conforms that , all employees needs consisted of a satisfying working environment, training and career development opportunities, reward and recognition, good pay and conditions, good working relationships, good resources – state of the art equipment, status, challenging job and autonomy. However it is unable to address and satisfy the needs all employees due to limited resources.

Core employees will be singled out by management for special treatment in terms financial compensation to certain extent. In summary, participants highlighted several salient needs of core employees and they included satisfactory work environment, training and career development opportunities, challenging assignments and pay, reward and recognition. In order to examine person organization-fit trends of the company, participants were asked on the hiring practices weather it influence the retention of employees. The company has clear polices on employee recruitment and selection. But it was not properly implemented. The award system and industrial environment is very restrictive. That is awards are job specific and do not facilitate multi-skilling through different award coverage, developed within a confrontational, negative, litigious framework. As such, they do not facilitate flexible arrangements that assist in skill and knowledge development.

Generally from the Pay strategies seek to not only attract but retain core personnel, particularly there is a clear link between intellectual capital of the individual and the firm's competitiveness overall, the experts' comments revealed some mixed concerns about the influence of HRM on retention. The constraints highlighted included the lack of importance placed on the role of HRM, the impact of industrial relations regulations and the application of fragmented functions diminished its impact. The level of responsibility and ability to utilize and develop skills in the company for the last few years wear under standard. Employees were not considered as assets of the company; rather they considered as cost of the company.

What they lack for the last few years was influential and sensitive leadership, company policies and culture, communication and consultation, effective integration of working relationships and satisfactory working environment. This highly affects the motivation and productivity of employees in the company and consequently involuntary turnover was increased from year to year. It is clear that employees would remain in an organization due to a satisfying working environment: suitable work conditions and good workmates provide comfort and security needed to support work activity. A quality of working life that allows sufficient monetary reward to meet individuals' needs, challenging work and a workload that allows balance for individuals' lifestyle needs to be met according to the participants.

Leadership management relates to sound supervision and direction: clear work standards, good instructions on how to do the job, objective performance assessment and an influential and sensitive leadership style from supervisor/manager provides an understandable and acceptable context in which to get jobs done as required based on the discussions of the participants. With regards to communication and consultation, most of the respondents stated that: quality and timeliness of feedback to employees is the hallmark of an effective organization. The participants were strongly commented that employees should be identified as a key resource and of strategic value to the company. They also highlighted the importance of managing and retaining this valued human capital. Employees' needs are focused on remuneration, training and development, career advancement, challenging job, growth opportunities and recognition of their capabilities and acquisition of new skills. Those needs should be take in to consideration to retained effective and capable employees.

As a consequence of the changes in the relationship between employers and employees there is a need to examine the human resource systems that support this primary labour force. The relationship between retention and human resource management factors and organizational factor were also discussed by the participants. They identified some key HR and organizational factors influencing retention. The factors identified by the FGD included selection, reward and recognition, training and career development, challenging job opportunities, equity of compensation, leadership style, company culture and culture, communication and consultation, effective working relationships and satisfactory work environment. This belief is supported by studies of progressive HRM practices in training, compensation and reward sharing. These studies have revealed that these can lead to reduced turnover and absenteeism, better quality work, and better financial performance (Arthur 1994). From the discussion; the following points were summarized as findings of the FGD.

- There is no employee Retention Strategy and succession plan

- All most all human resource principles and management approaches were not properly implemented; due to this significant number of employees were resign from the factory

- The policies and principles of the factory were not properly executed as a result the transparency and accountability in recruitment and selection process were under problem.

- The reward and compensation program of the factory was not timely revised like other competitive companies.

- Opportunities of to date training and development for employees also another factor for turn over

- The style of leadership was not allow employees to create/ develop work place team relationship and for friendly working environment

- Employees were not recognized and acknowledge for their contribution periodically.

Finally to assure the sustainability of the issue understudy(employee retention strategy) the participants point out that alignment of HRM with company strategy raises an interesting inquiry of Dashen Brewery to consider retaining their valued employees as a strategic issue and a competitive advantage.

Chapter five

Findings, Conclusion, and Recommendation

Findings

As witnessed by the quantitative and qualitative (FGD) results of this study; all most all human resource principles and management approaches were not properly implemented. More over due to the absence of due attention to the human capital of the factory significant number of employees were resign from the factory. All in all the following points were identified as findings of the project .the outcome of this project.

Recruitment is one of the key aspects for retention. If the selection process is deficient, it can lead to employees leaving earlier than their employer would like them to, thus increasing turnover costs. It could also allow poor performers enter and stay in the organization, driving down its performance. However, the above facts were not having a place on employee recruitment and selection in Dashen Brewery. Selection and placing were practiced un-transparently by the willingness of some individual who has organizational power to do so.

One of the major reasons why people resign is when they feel that they have stopped learning and developing personally or professionally. The employer obviously has a key role to play to ensure that its employees are faced with new challenging tasks and equipped with the skills necessary to deal with their work. But creating training and career development opportunities were not a culture of Dashen Brewery. Accordingly this practice was negatively influence the commitment and motivation of employee to stay in the company.

One concern of staff is work-life balance, something increasingly important to individuals. Agreeing on such an issue requires consultation and dialogue to accommodate individual preferences, dialogue with staff on matters likely to affect their employment enhances the quality and effectiveness of our policies and practices. As I observed from the focus group discussion, the potential case of turnover of employees were due to the dictatorial leadership style of employee management relationship and null right of free deem of expression what they fill related to their work.

Good support, management and leadership of staff are a key for the effectiveness the factory. Managers are also often the factor that will make the difference between staying and resigning. According to the participants of the FGD, the human resource management trends of the factory were not addressed the concerns of employees. They also confirm that employees were not considered as source of competitive advantage for the factory rather they were considered as cost of the company and employee issues were not seen as the issues of the company Due to this fact, the company has no any employee retention management strategy.

Another key finding of this study is there is strong correlation between demographic factors and intention to stay. However the study points out that woman are relatively more committed to organizations than male. This research provided evidence that older employees and individuals with more seniority within the organization were less likely to report they planned to resign.

Another findings of the study demonstrates that commitment can be influenced by bundles of HR factors (i.e. selection (person organization fit), remuneration, reward and recognition, training and career development, challenging assignments) and Organizational factors (i.e. leadership behavior, organizational culture and policies, teamwork relationship and satisfactory work environment.) Moreover, commitment acts as a partial mediator of the relationship between remuneration, recognition and reward, training and career development and work environment on intent to stay. Commitment fully mediates the relationship between person

70

organization fit, teamwork relationship, culture and policies and intention to stay.

In summary, the findings of the study put forward that retention can be influenced by selection (person organization fit), remuneration, reward and recognition, training and career development, challenging assignments. However in Dashen Brewery leadership behavior, organizational culture and policies, teamwork relationship and satisfactory work environment have strong significant impact on employees' decision of stay. The result of the project demonstrated that the relationships between human resource factor and turnover intention have produced few large correlations. One explanation for the low commitment-turnover correlations is that other variables probably moderate this relationship.

Conclusion

Based on the findings of the project the potential causes of employee turnover in Dashen Brewery was mainly due to the leadership practice, reward &recognition and absence of opportunities for career development. But this does not mean that other HR and organizational factors were not having an impact on employee turnover. No actions were made to control employee turnover rates. There was no employee's retention strategy in the company. In light of the focus group discussion and the quantitative survey result; there is a change in the overall management style s of the company and the management was trying to address the issue of employees to minimize employee turnover and to boost the morals' of employees for better productivity. Additionally, Staff encouragement is an inexpensive way to boost employee morale and commitment to his/her work. Larson and Hewitt (2005) state that it is important to recognize good work both verbally and formally. The literature indicates that while it is important to correct negative behavior it is equally important to point out good work. A simple verbal praise or note from a management can make a big difference in an employee's morale and sense of belonging to the factory. Recognizing well performers and displaying their name and department on the notice board could lead to better morale. Other gestures such as gift certificates on the company's anniversary date might also increase the commitment and productivity of employees.

The result reveal that both HRM and organizational factor/s influence employees' decisions to stay. In all, it appears that the relationship between HR factors, organizational factors and intention to stay is conditional upon commitment. The findings of the study also confirmed a significant relationship between organizational commitment and intent to stay. It also shows that a both HR factors and organizational factors had a relationship to one another.

The correlation tests indicated that there is a positive relationship between training and career development with employee intention to stay.

The result shows that positive significant co-relationships between the eight factors and organizational commitment. These specific factors consisted of two bundles of practices: HR factors (e.g. person organizational fit, remuneration, reward and recognition, training and career development, challenging job opportunities) and Organizational factors (e.g. leadership behavior, company culture and policies, teamwork relationship and satisfactory work environment).

Moreover, commitment acts as a moderator of remuneration, recognition and reward, training and career development and work environment on intent to stay. Commitment also mediates person organization fit, teamwork relationship, culture and policies on intention to stay. Of particular interest however is that commitment acts as a mediator between the factors identified and intent to stay.

Of particular importance was the demonstration that the relationship between selection (person organization fit), teamwork relationship, organizational culture and policies to intention to stay is mediated by commitment acts as a partial mediator of the relationship between work environment, remuneration, recognition and reward, training and career development and intention to stay.

The multiple regression data analysis test did show statistical significance determines what HR and organizational factors are more influential for employees decision of stay. Thus, in Dashen Brewery organizational factor bundle more critical and significant for employees' decision of stay. Particularly leadership behavior has greater value of beta compare to other factors. The current management bodies of the factory were aware on the reasons of employee turnover and due to this they are devising some remedial actions to retain productive employees in the company. One of the indication of their measure were identifying

72

researchable topic for this project to have scientific based findings and recommendations related to employee retention management.

Leadership practice, Employability, rapid change on the reward and compensation structure of competitive firms, unbalanced understanding and awareness on the importance of employee retention among management members, and the location of the firms were identified as major challenges to retained employees in the company.

The effectiveness of any HR practice or set of practices for impacting firm performance depends upon the firm's strategy (or conversely, the effectiveness of any strategy depends upon having the right HR practices). Thus, from a practical perspective, the project offers a HRM retention strategic solution for organizations. If properly implemented, the "bundles" of HR and organizational factors identified in this project will ensure an alignment between HR and business strategy to gain competitive advantage over the company's human capital.

Recommendation

From the results presented above several recommendations can be derived for successful employee retention management program of Dashen Brewery. Based on the analysis, discussions and findings of the project study with refereeing to the review of the literature; the following points are forwarded as recommendation which will help to solve the identified gap related to employee retention management and to foster better retention practices in Dashen Brewery plc. They are presented as follows:

❖ **Apply total quality Human resource management trends:** Total quality human resources management (TQHRM) is "an approach to human resources management that involves many of the concepts of quality management." The primary goal of TQHRM is employee empowerment. The full potential of employee empowerment is realized in the empowered organization, when employees: align their goals with appropriate higher organization purpose; have the authority and opportunity to maximize their contribution; are capable of taking appropriate action; are committed to the organization's purpose; and have the means to achieve it. Empowerment requires the alignment, authority, capability, and commitment of employees. In order to achieve these goals, the following steps must be taken to achieve each goal.

➢ **Alignment** . Alignment can be realized if employees:

• Know the needs of customers and stakeholders

• Know, concur in, and be prepared to contribute effort to organization strategies, goals, objectives, and plans

➢ **Authority** . In order for employees to the have the authority and opportunity to contribute to the organization, the following steps are required:

• Individual authority, responsibility, and capability are consistent

• Barriers to successful exercise of authority have been removed

• The necessary tools and support are in place

➢ **Capability** . Employee capability can be developed through:

• Organizational training initiatives

• Educational development

➢ **Commitment.** An organization must earn the commitment of employees through:

• Reinforcement

• Recognition

• Rewards

Figure 7 TQHRM processes

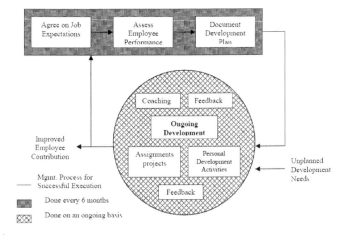

❖ **Selecting proper leadership style**: Transformational leadership is used to help the subordinates aware that rewards need making efforts. Proper encouragement and consideration are required to raise the eager for future vision and accomplishment of mutual goal. The personality of the leader has significant impact on employees' decision to stay or leave. Personality characteristic is a combination of individual trait and property, which generates a lasting and special characteristic different from the others. It also means one's psychological and physical phenomenon. At different time and condition, it adapts to different environment by unique behavioral mode and thinking method. Friedman & Rosenman (1959) categorize personality characteristics into type A and B. Type A shows exuberant ambition and aggression. Type B has more patience and pays less attention to competition and sense of achievement. The leader should spend more time in assistance and communication so that the subordinates can be motivated and enhanced their level of commitment.

✓ *To uplift the knowhow of the management; it is better to give a one day training on "**the impact of leadership style and leader personalities on employee retention and company performance**"*

The contents of the training will be:
  ➤ *Understanding organizational behavior form real experience*
  ➤ *Types of leadership and its impact on company performance*
  ➤ *Meaning of personality and its contribution*
  ➤ *Types of personality and its characteristics*
  ➤ *The big five personality traits*

❖ **Clear understanding and awareness:** the management should understand the overall impact of employee turnover on the company's performance and productivity. the following points can help the impact of turn over;

Calculating Employee Turnover Rates

For the last 12-month period, add up the number of terminations. Next divide by the total number of employees at the end of the same 12-month period.

That is;

$$\text{Turnover rate} = \frac{\text{Total Number of termination}}{\text{Total Number of employees}} \times 100$$

$$= \underline{\hspace{4cm}}\%$$

Calculating Direct Turnover Costs

1. Costs Due to a Person Leaving

a. Estimate the cost of the person(s) who fills in while the position is vacant. This can be either the cost of a temporary or the cost of existing employees performing the vacant job along with their own. Tally this figure using overtime rates.

b. Calculate the cost of lost productivity at a minimum of 50% of the person's compensation and benefits for each week the position is vacant, even if there are people performing the work. Figure the lost productivity at 100% if the position is completely vacant for any period of time.

c. Compute the cost of an exit interview to include the time of the person conducting the interview; the time of the person leaving; the administrative expense of stopping payroll, benefit deductions, and benefit enrollments; notification and administration; and time spent on various forms needed to process a resigning employee.

d. Estimate the cost of the manager understanding what work remains and how to cover that work until a replacement is found. Calculate the expense of the manager conducting their own version of the employee exit interview.

e. Tally the cost of the training your company has invested in the employee who is leaving. Include internal training, external programs, and external academic education. Include licenses or certifications the company has helped the employee obtain to do their job effectively.

f. Determine the impact on departmental productivity because the person is leaving. Who will pick up the work, whose work will suffer, and what departmental deadlines will not be met? Consider the cost of department staff discussing their reactions to the vacancy.

g. Calculate the cost of severance and benefits continuation provided to employees who are leaving that are eligible for coverage under those programs.

h. Tally the cost of lost knowledge, skills, and contacts that the departing person is taking out of your door. Use a formula of 50% of the person's annual salary for one year of service, increasing this figure for each year employed by 10%.

i. Determine the cost impact of unemployment insurance premiums as well as the time spent to prepare for an unemployment hearing, or the cost paid to a third party to handle the unemployment claim process on your behalf.

j. Estimate the cost of losing customers that the employee is going to take with them, or the amount it will cost you to retain the customers of the sales person or customer service representative who leaves.

k. Subtract the cost of the departing person for the amount of time the position is vacant.

2. Recruitment Costs

77

a. Consider the cost of advertisements (from a $200 classified to a $5,000+ display advertisement); agency costs at 20 - 30% of annual compensation; employee referral costs of $500 - $2,000 or more; Internet posting costs of $300 - $500 per listing.

b. Tally the cost of the internal recruiter's time to understand the position requirements, develop and implement a sourcing strategy, review candidates' backgrounds, prepare for interviews, conduct interviews, prepare candidate assessments, conduct reference checks, make the employment offer, and notify unsuccessful candidates. This can range from a minimum of 30 hours to over 100 hours per position.

c. Calculate the cost of a recruiter's assistant who will spend 20 or more hours in basic level review of resumes, developing candidate interview schedules, and making any travel arrangements for out-of-town candidates.

d. Determine the cost of hiring (immediate supervisor, next level manager, peers, and other people on the selection committee) including time to review and explain position requirements, review the background of candidates, conduct interviews, discuss their assessments, and select a finalist. Also include their time to do their own sourcing of candidates from networks, contacts, and other referrals. This can take upwards of 100 hours of total time.

e. Add up the administrative cost of handling, processing, and responding to the average number of resumes considered for each opening at $1.50 per resume.

f. Calculate the number of hours spent by the internal recruiter interviewing internal candidates along with the cost of those internal candidates being away from their jobs while interviewing.

g. Estimate the cost of drug screens, educational and criminal background checks, and other reference checks, especially if these tasks are outsourced. Don't forget to calculate the number of times these are done per open position as some companies conduct this process for the final two or three candidates.

h. Consider the cost of the various candidate pre-employment tests that help assess candidates' skills, abilities, aptitude, attitude, values, and behaviors.

3. Training Costs

a. Calculate the cost of the orientation and the cost of the person who conducts the orientation. Also include the cost of orientation materials.

b. Determine the cost of departmental training as the actual development and delivery cost plus the cost of the salary of the new employee. Note that the cost will be significantly higher for some positions such as sales representatives and call center agents who require four to six weeks or more of classroom training.

c. Figure the cost of the person(s) who conducts the training.

d. Tally the cost of various training materials needed including company or product manuals, computer or other technology equipment used in the delivery of training.

e. Calculate the cost of supervisory time spent in assigning, explaining, and reviewing work assignments and output. This represents lost productivity of the supervisor. Estimate the amount of time spent at seven hours per week for at least eight weeks.

4. Lost Productivity Costs

As the new employee is learning the job, the company policies and practices, etc., they are not fully productive. Use the following guidelines to calculate the cost of this lost productivity:

a. Upon completion of whatever training is provided, the employee is contributing at a 25% productivity level for the first two to four weeks. The cost therefore is 75% of the new employee's full salary during that time period.

b. During the fifth through the twelfth week, the employee is contributing at a 50% productivity level. The cost is therefore 50% of full salary during that time period.

c. During the thirteenth through the twentieth week, the employee is contributing at a 75% productivity level. The cost is therefore 25% of full salary during that time period.

d. Calculate the cost of coworkers and supervisory lost productivity due to their time spent on bringing the new employee "up to speed."

e. Figure the cost of mistakes the new employee makes during this elongated indoctrination period.

f. Estimate the cost of lost department productivity caused by a departing member of management who is no longer available to guide and direct the remaining staff.

g. Calculate the impact cost on the completion or delivery of a critical project where the departing employee is a key participant.

h. Tally the cost of reduced productivity of a manager or director who loses a key staff member, such as an assistant, who handled a great deal of routine, administrative tasks that the manager will now have to handle.

5. New Hire Costs

a. Calculate the cost of bringing the new person on board including the cost to put the person on the payroll, establish computer and security passwords and identification cards, business cards, internal and external publicity announcements, telephone hookups, cost of establishing e-mail accounts, the expense of establishing credit card accounts, or leasing other equipment such as cell phones, automobiles, pagers.

b. Figure the expense of a manager's time spent developing trust and building confidence in the new employee's work.

6. Lost Sales Costs

a. For sales staff, divide the budgeted revenue per sales territory into weekly amounts and multiply that amount for each week the territory is vacant, including training time. Also use the lost productivity calculations above to estimate the lost sales until the sales representative is fully productive. This can also be used for telemarketing and inside sales representatives.

b. For non-sales staff, calculate the revenue per employee by dividing total company revenue by the average number of employees in a given year. Whether an employee contributes directly or indirectly to the generation of revenue, their purpose is to provide some defined set of responsibilities that are necessary to the generation of revenue. Estimate the lost revenue by multiplying the number of weeks the position is vacant by the average weekly revenue per employee. Look the following table, it represents summary of some of direct cost of employee turnover.

Cost items	Cost in Birr
Recruiting Cost	
Advertising, radio, direct mail etc.	
Interviewing Costs (time spent x the wage of the interviewer)	
Interviewing	
Reference Checks	
Exit Interview (time spent x the wage of the processor)	
Administrative Costs (time spent x the wage of the administrator)	
Processing of paper work for newly hired employee	
Processing of paper work of exiting employee	
Uniform Costs	
Supervision Costs (Time spent x the wages of the manager)	

Training Costs	
Time spent training (xx hrs.) x wage of employee	
Time spent training (xx hrs.) x wage of trainer	
Materials, equipment, job aids	
Separation of Costs	
Average cost of unemployment, separation pay, legal claims	
Overtime costs to do work of exiting employee	
Total for Direct Costs	

Turnover costs also take into account **indirect costs.** Research indicates that the indirect costs of turnover can be 2 to 5 times higher than direct costs. These costs are more difficult to quantify and assign a dollar figure to, but they are very real.

◈ **Competitive and Fair Compensation/internal equity**   to maintain productive employees in the factory there should be competitive and faire compensation policy. Internal equity in compensation refers to comparisons employees make to other employees within the same organization. In making these comparisons employees question whether they are being equitably paid for their contributions to the organization relative to the way other employees in the organization are paid.

◈ **Adequate and Flexible Benefits** can demonstrate to employees that a company is supportive and fair, and there is evidence to suggest that benefits are at the top of the list of reasons why employees choose to stay with their employer or to join the company in the first place. Flexibility in benefits packages can enhance retention, as it creates responsiveness to the specific needs and circumstances of individual employees.

◈ **Innovative Compensation Systems** and practices can have a positive impact on employee retention by motivating membership-oriented behavior (commitment). Pay systems may also affect knowledge sharing and transfer if sharing, teamwork, suggestions, etc. are rewarded or recognized. Innovative compensation systems include gain sharing, skill-based pay and various types of bonus plans. There are four basic design elements for linking bonuses to competencies. These are;

82

1. Competency-related certification standards
2. Guidelines for bonus award amounts
3. Timing of award consideration
4. Linkage to performance appraisal results

❖ **Recognition and Rewards** include a diverse range of formal and informal, financial and non-financial incentives given to individual employees, groups of employees or to an entire staff. They include such things as employee of the month awards, company-sponsored sports teams and social events, prizes, clothing, and so on. Recognition and rewards can contribute to a workplace culture of respect and appreciation for employees and work well done, and thereby reinforce employee commitment to the firm. Thus the company has advice to celebrate employees' day annually.

The Five Most Important Tips for Effective Recognition

You need to establish criteria for what performance or contribution constitutes reward able behavior or actions.

- *All employees must be eligible for the recognition.*
- *The recognition must supply the employer and employee with specific information about what behaviors or actions are being rewarded and recognized.*
- *Anyone who then performs at the level or standard stated in the criteria receives the reward.*
- *The recognition should occur as close to the performance of the actions as possible, so the recognition reinforces behavior the employer wants to encourage.*
- *You don't want to design a process in which managers "select" the people to receive recognition. This type of process will be viewed forever as "favoritism" or talked about as "it's your turn to get recognized this month." This is why processes that single out an individual, such as "Employee of the Month," are rarely effective.*

❖ **Training, Professional Development, and Career Planning** to enhance employees' organizational citizen ship and commitment, to bring direct positive impact on employee retention there should be regular training, professional development, career planning and succession plan for prospective mangers. For this purpose there should be training and development officer or the personnel officer has to be responsible. Training need assessment should be conducted periodically and reported to the concerned body on time (see Annex C).

83

◈ **Recruitment & Orientation** practices can be of crucial importance to make workers stay over a longer time. Employee retention is enhanced by ensuring a good "fit" between a company's workplace cultures. Recruitment practices that emphasize not only formal qualifications (job-relevant technical ability) but also more general types of qualifications and dispositions on the part of the recruit can be part of an effective retention strategy. Good initial orientation to the newly-hired employee can not only help to effectively integrate that person into the workplace but can also help to make the new person feel welcome and provide him or her information about how to cope with the demands of the workplace, and any possible problems that may arise.

◈ **Healthy Workplace or Wellness Initiatives** take on a variety of forms, including those directed at the physical work environment (cleanliness, safety, ergonomics, etc.); health practices (supporting healthy lifestyles, fitness, diet, etc.); and social environment and personal resources (organizational culture, a sense of control over one's work, employee assistance programs, etc.). Healthy workplace initiatives not only improve the health and well-being of individual employees, but contribute to business performance objectives including employee retention.

◈ **Employee Participation & Communication:** Open, responsive, two-way communications are vital to good employee retention, and should be considered as the basic building blocks of any effective retention practice. Most, if not all, of the retention strategies and practices fundamentally depend on a sound approach to communicating with employees. Without communications, many of these practices would be impossible to implement in any effective way. The company keeps their employees regularly up to date on the company's financial performance, and maintains open-door communication policies.

◈ **Job Design & Work Teams** can enhance the intrinsic rewards of the job, making work more fulfilling, challenging, interesting, and stimulating. Practices such as autonomous or semi-autonomous work teams, 'self-scheduling,' and job rotation can not only improve retention but have also been shown to improve a number of other important indicators such as productivity, accidents and injuries and product quality.

◈ **Knowledge Transfer   cross-training, coaching and mentoring, phased in retirement.** While employee retention practices seek to retain workers, knowledge transfer practices seek to retain skills, through both formal and informal exercises in information sharing and the building of collective knowledge. Mentoring and coaching, phased-in retirements, and cross-training and job rotation, are types of knowledge transfer that overlap with training. Knowledge transfer also includes the use of technology-based tools—databases, intranets, groupware—aimed to support knowledge sharing among individuals, and to permanently document and keep knowledge that is vital to business performance.

◈ **Relationship training and recognition of employees should be implemented.**
When an employee is trained by their supervising staff, generally a better relationship is formed between those two employees. On-going training should also be established in order to promote confidence in staff. When an individual feels confident in their abilities they are more motivated in their position. Providing direct care staff with advanced knowledge of their job tasks, as well as, other related skills such as sign language or sensitivity training can help to motivate employees to perform better and ultimately increase retention rates (Larson and Hewitt, 2008).

◈ **Further investigation to gain a better understanding of why employees leave the factory:** The Company should conduct additional research to determine what other variables can account for employee turnover rates of Dashen Brewery. It would be important for the factory to gain a better understanding of the reasons employees leave the organization; I would suggest that exit interviews are conducted and evaluated on a regular basis. The termination reports that have been collected through exit interview will offer a basic understanding of why employees leave Dashen, more detailed reports might offer additional insight into how employees would be retained. Exit interviews should be distributed when an employee is dropping off their badge and keys so that the response rate will be as high as possible (see annex D).

The company should also continue to monitor the satisfaction and fillings of current employees. Small focus groups from each department may be another way for the factory to collect data about the overall causes and motivating factors for employee retention. Additional research focused on proactive approaches to motivating current employees will increase the productive life of the factory. Feasibility studies on such measures as changing current evaluation of employees might be another avenue for Dashen to explore.

Summary

This paper contributes to the scarce research on how Dashen Brewery's can retain employees for better productivity and competitive advantage. It sought to find out; cause of employee turnover and Dashen Brewery's retention strategy, examine employee turnover management practice, spot which HRM and organizational factors influence employees' decisions to stay. It also examined the relationships between the HR factor bundle, organizational factor bundle, organizational commitment and intention to stay and identify which factors are most critical for employee retention.

Employee retention is one of the principal problems that Dashen Brewery currently faces. In order to provide high quality services to clients, the factory must retain an adequate number of well trained employees. The high cost of training new staff, as well as service diminishment, make turnover one of the most pressing issues for Dashen. In an attempt to understand what factors motivate employees to stay at Dashen Brewery this project was conducted at the factory.

The project examined the retention strategy of the company in light of human resource factor bundle and organizational factor bundle. The data which were collected through questionnaires and FGD were assessed using a variety of statistical tools in order to gain insight into which dimensions affected employee retention more significantly.

It examines   the relationships among HR factor bundle, organizational factor bundle organizational commitment, and turnover intention (intent to stay). Organizational commitment and intention to stay (turnover intention) were selected as the focal dependent variables to examine the strategy and practice of employee retention strategy. The findings of this project revealed positive significant co-relationships between the factors and intention to stay. These factors consisted of two bundles of practices: HR factors (e.g., person organizational fit,

86

remuneration, reward and recognition, training and career development, challenging job opportunities) and Organizational factors (e.g. leadership behavior, company culture and policies, teamwork relationship, communication and satisfactory work environment).

Reference

Abbasi, S., & Hollman, K. (2000). Turnover: The Real Bottom-line. *Public Personnel Management, 29*(3), 333-342.

Accenture, (2001).'The high performance workforce: separating the digital economy's winners from losers.' In The Battle for Retention Accenture's study, pp. 1-5.

Allen, N. (1996). 'Affective, continuance, and normative commitment to the organisation: an examination of construct validity'. Journal of Vocational Behaviour , December, v49 n3, pp. 252- 76.

Anand, K.N. (1997). 'Give success a chance.' Quality Progress, March, pp. 63-64.

Arthur, J. (1994), 'Effects of human resource systems on manufacturing performance and turnover.' In Academy of Management Journal, v37, pp. 670-87.

Barney, J.B. (1991). 'Firm resources and sustained competitive advantage.' In Journal of Management, March, v17, pp. 99-120.

Baron, R.M. and Kenny, D.A.(1986). 'The moderator-mediator variable distinction in Social Psychological Research: conceptual, Strategic and statistical considerations.' In Journal of Personality of Social Psychological, v51, n6, pp.1173-82.

Bass, B.M. and Avolio, B.J. (1995). The Multifactor Leadership Questionnaire. Mind Garden, Paolo Alto, CA.

Beck, S. (2001). 'Why Associates Leave, and Strategies To Keep Them.' In American Lawyer Media L.P., v5, i2, pp. 23-27.

Becker, B. and Gerhart, B. (1996), 'The impact of human resource management on organisational performance: Progress and prospects.' In Academy of Management Journal, v39, pp. 779-801.

Becker, B.E. and Huselid, M.A. (1998), 'High performance work systems and firm performance: A synthesis of research and managerial implications.' In Personnel and Human Resource Management, v16, pp. 53-101.

Berenson, M. L. and Levine D. M. (1996). Basic business statistics: Concepts and applications. (6th Edition.) Englewood Cliffs, NJ: Prentice Hall.

Bryman, A. (1992). Charisma and Leadership in Organisations. Sage Publications, Newbury, C.A.

Clarke, K.F. (2001). 'What businesses are doing to attract and retain employee—becoming an employer of choice.' In Employee Benefits Journal, March, pp. 34-37.

Comrey, A.L. and Lee, H.B. (1992). A First Course in Factor Analysis. (2 edition). Hillsdale, NJ: Erlbaum. Nd ,pp 23-28

Davies, R, (2001,). 'How to boost Staff Retention.' In People Management, v7, i8, April 19, pp. 54-56.

Davis, D. (1996). Business Research for Decision Making. 4 edition, Belmont, CA: Wadsworth Publishing.

Delaney, J. and Huselid, M. (1996). 'The impact of HRM practices on perceptions of organisational performance.' In Academy of Management Journal, v39, pp. 949-69.

Delery, J.E. (1998). 'Issues of fit in strategic human resource management: implications for research.' In Human Resource Management Review, v8, pp. 289-309.

Delery, J.E. and Doty, D.H. 1996. 'Theoretical frameworks in strategic human resource management: Universalistic, contingency and configurational perspectives.' In Academy of Management Journal , v39, pp. 802-35.

Eskildesn, J.K. and Nussler, M.L. (2000). 'The managerial drivers of employee satisfaction and loyalty.' In Total Quality Management, July, pp. 581 - 90.

Fitz-enz, J (1997). 'The passionate leader.' Measuring Business Excellence, v1, n2, pp. 5

Fitz-enz, J. (1990). 'Getting and keeping good employees.' In Personnel, August, v67, n8, pp. 25-29.

Frazis, H., Gittleman, M., Horrigan, M. and Joyce, M. (1998). 'Results from the 1995 Survey of Employer-Provided Training.' In Monthly Labor Review, June, v121, n6, pp. 3-14.

Gorhart. K and Bedcer   S. (2000). 'Career experiences, perceptions of employment practices, and psychological commitment in the organisation.' In Human Relations, v42, n11, pp. 35

Gramm, C.L. and Schnell, J.F (2001). 'The Use of Flexible staffing arrangements in core production jobs.' In Industrial and Labor Relations Review, Jan, v54, i2, pp. 245 - 251.

Hale, G. (1989). 'Strategic intent.' In Harvard Business Review, v67, n3, pp. 63-76.

Hair .P , Miller, V.D and Johnson, J.R. (1992). 'Socialisation, resocialisation, and communication relationships in the context of an organisational change.' In Communication Studies , Winter, v54, i4, pp. 483-96.

Hayes, C. (1998). 'Business Dynamos.' Black Enterprise August , v29, n1 pp.58-64.

Huselid, M. A. (1995). 'The impact of human resource management practices on turnover, productivity, and corporate financial performance.' In Academy of Management Journal, v38, pp. 635-72.

Jackson, P.R., Wall, T.D., Martin, R. and Davids, K. (1993). 'New measures of job control, cognitive demand and production responsibility.' In Journal of Applied Psychology , v78, n5, pp. 753-62.

Jackson, S.E. and Schuler, R.S. (1995). 'Understanding human resource management in the context of organisations and their environments. In Annual Review of Psychology, ed. J.T. Spence, J.M. Darley and D.J. Foss, v46, pp. 237-64. Palo Alto, CA: Annual Reviews.

Kane, R. (2000). 'Downsizing, TQM, reengineering, learning organisations and HRM strategy.' In Asia Pacific Journal of Management, v38, n1, pp. 26-48.

Kaye, Beverley and Sharon Jordan-Evans. Love 'Em or Lose 'Em: Getting Good People to Stay (San Francisco: Berret-Koehler, 1999).

Koene, B.A., Boone, C.A.J.J., Soeters J.L. (1997). 'Organisational factors influencing homogeneity and heterogeneity of organisational cultures.' In Cultural Complexity in Organisations: Inherent Contrasts and Contradictions, ed. Sackmann S.A., Thousand Oaks, CA: Sage. pp. 273-93.

Larson, S. A., & Hewitt, A.S.(2005). Staff recruitment, retention & training strategies for community human service organizations. Baltimore: Paul H. Brooks publishing company. pp 23-34

Lawler, E. (1992). The Ultimate Advantage: Creating the High-Involvement Organisation. San Francisco: Jossey-Bass.

Lawson, T.E. and Hepp, R.L. (2000). 'Measuring the performance impact of human resource initiatives.' In Human Resource Planning, New York, v24, i2, pp. 36-45.

Lee, T.W., Ashford, S.J., Walsh, J.P. and Mowday, R.T. (1992). 'Commitment propensity, organisational commitment, and voluntary turnover: a longitudinal study of organisational entry processes.' In Journal of Management, v18, pp. 15-26.

Likert, R. (1961). New Patterns of Management. New York; McGraw-Hill.

MacDuffie, J. (1995). 'Human resource bundles and manufacturing performance: organisational logic and flexible production systems in the world auto industry.' In Industrial and Labor Relations Review , v48, pp. 197-221.

Marchington, M. and Wilkinson, A. (1997). Core Personnel and Development.   London, Institute of Personnel and Development.

Mercer Report,(2003). Mercer study raises red flags for employer pay and benefit plans (findings of the 2002 People at work survey). In Human Resource Department Management Report, May, pp. 8-15.

Milory, L. (2004). 'The people make the process: commitment to employees, decision making, and performance.' In Journal of Management, March, v27, i2, pp. 163 - 65.

Mowday, R.T., Steers, R.M. and Porter, L.W. (1979). 'The measurement of organisational commitment.' In Journal of Vocational Behavior, v14, pp. 224-47.

Netemeyer, R.G., Boles, J.S., McKee, D.O. and McMurrian, R. (1997) 'An investigation into the antecedents of organisational citizenship behaviors in a personal selling context.' In Journal   of Marketing, v61, pp. 85-98.

Noe, R.A. (1999). Employee Training and Development. New York   : Irwin McGraw-Hill.

Osterman, P. (1994). How common is workplace transformation and who adopts it? Industrial and Labour Relations Review, v47, n2, pp.173-88.

Ostroff, C. and Bowen, D.E. (2000). 'Moving HR to a higher level: HR practices and organisational effectiveness.' In Multilevel theory, research, and methods in organisations: foundations, extensions, and new directions, ed. K.J. Klein and S.W.J. Kozlowski, San Francisco: Jossey-Bass, pp. 211-66.

Parker, O. and Wright, L. (2000). 'Pay and employee commitment: the missing link.' In Ivey Business Journal, Jan, v65, i3, pp. 70   - 79.

Pfeffer, J. (1994). Competitive Advantage Through People: Unleashing the Power of the Work Force. Boston: Harvard Business School Press.

Phillips, R. (1997). 'New measures for business.' In Measuring Business Excellence, v1, n1, pp. 4-7.

Podsakoff, P.M., MacKenzie, S.B., and Bommer, W.H. (1996). 'Transformational leader behaviours and substitutes for   leadership as determinants of employee satisfaction, commitment, trust and organisational citizenship behaviours.' In Journal of Management , v22, pp. 259-98.

Porter, M.V. (2001). 'The bottom line in employee compensation.' In Association Management , April, v53, i4, pp. 44-50.

Ramlall.M.(2003). 'The consequences of organizational commitment: Methodological investigation.' Journal of Organisational Behavior, v11, pp. 361-78.

Shepherd, J.L. and Mathews, B.P. (2000). 'Employee commitment: academic vs. practitioner perspectives.' Employee Relations, v22, pp. 555-75.

Shore, L.M. and Wayne, S.J. (1993). 'Commitment and employee behaviour.' In Journal of Applied Psychology , v78, pp. 774-80.

Smith V. (1997). 'New forms of work organisation.' In Annual Review Sociology, v23, pp. 315-39.

Snell, S. and Dean, J. (1992). 'Integrated manufacturing and human resource management: a human capital perspective.' In Academy of Management Journal, v35, pp. 467-504.

Solomon, C.M. (1999). 'Brace for change.' In Workforce, January, v78, i1, pp. 6-11.

Tabachnick, B.G. and Fidell, L.S. (2001). Using Multivariate Statistics.   (4 edition), New York: Harper Collins College Publishers.

Walker, J.W. (2001). 'Perspectives' Human Resource Planning, March v24, i1, pp. 6-10.

Willis, C. (2000). 'Go for your goals. Working Woman, March, pp. 6-7.

Yammarino, F.J. and Bass, B.M, (1990). 'Transformational leadership and multiple levels of analysis.' Human Relations, v43, pp. 975-95.

Zikmud (1997). Minimizing turnover among support counselors through a value based culture. *Journal for Nonprofit Management, Volume 11.* Retrieved Feb 03, 2009, frohttp://www.supportctr.org/images/minimizingturnover.pdf.

This page has been intentionally left blank.

This page has been intentionally left blank.

Annexes

Anex A: Questionnaire

Addis Ababa University
School of Commerce
Post graduate studies
Master of Art in Human Resource Management (MA HRM)

An Examination of Employee Retention Management practices: A Case study in Dashen Brewery PLC

Part one
Questionnaire for Employees

By: Birhanu G/Silassie

Advisor: Wubshet Bekalu (PhD)

xi

Project Title: An Examination of Employee Retention Management practices: A Case study in Dashen Brewery PLC

To be filled by Employees of Dashen Brewery PLC

Dear Employee,

This questionnaire is designed to collect information about employee retention management practice of Dashen Brewery. The information shall be used as a primary data in the case research which has been conducting for partial requirement of for completing Master of Art in Human Resource Management (MA HRM) under Addis Ababa University School of commerce.

Retention of key personnel is a major Human Resource Management challenge facing most organizations of Ethiopia. This project will help to identify many issues, which could affect an individual's decision to stay with an employer. This study will help shape future human resource policies and assist in the development of an effective retention tool for your organization, as well as contribute to my project.

I would like to request your cooperation in completing the attached questionnaire. The questions seek your opinions regarding your company's human resource management practices in relation to retention issues. There is no right or wrong answers; we simply want your honest opinions. The survey will take approximately 15-20 minutes. If you have any questions regarding this project please feel free to contact myself, Birhanu G/Silassie, (at 0912 16 6579/09 18 08 18 88

E-maile: brshlink@gamile.com).

This questionnaire does not require you to personally identify yourself. Your information will remain anonymous and confidential and the data will only be reported in an aggregated form.

Thank you for your participation in this study. Your contribution is greatly appreciated.

Birhanu G/Silassie

Investigator

Part I: Human Resource Factors

The following statements relate to the way in which you perceive the human resource practices within your organization. For each statement, you are asked to mark an **X** in the box that best describes your response.

1. How accurately do the following statements best describe your personal fit with your company's culture and values?

1 Strongly Disagree	2 Disagree	3 Neither Agree nor Disagree	4 Agree	5 Strongly Agree				
	ORGANISATIONAL FIT			1	2	3	4	5
1	This organization has the same values as I do with regard to concern for others.							
2	This organization does not have the same value as I do with regard to fairness.							
3	This organization has the same values as I do with regard to honesty.							
4	I feel that my personal values are a good fit with this organizational culture.							

2. How accurately do the following statements describe your company's remuneration and recognition system?

1 Strongly Disagree	2 Disagree	3 Neither Agree nor Disagree	4 Agree	5 Strongly Agree				
	REMUNERATION AND RECOGNITION			1	2	3	4	5
5	Employees are given positive recognition when they produce high quality work							
6	This organization pays well.							
7	This organization offers a good benefits package compared to other organizations.							
8	This organization values individual excellence over teamwork.							
9	This organization offers good opportunities for Promotion.							

3. How accurately do the following statements describe your company's training and career development practices?

1 Strongly Disagree	2 Disagree	3 Neither Agree nor Disagree	4 Agree	5 Strongly Agree			
TRAINING AND CAREER DEVELOPMENT				1	2	3	4	5

		1	2	3	4	5
10	People are properly orientated and trained upon joining this organization.					
11	This organization does provide regular opportunities for personal and career development					
12	Innovation and creativity are encouraged here.					
13	The organization has career development activities to help an employee identify/ improve abilities, goals, strengths & weaknesses.					

4. How accurately do the following statements describe attributes that are currently present in your job?

1 Strongly Disagree	2 Disagree	3 Neither Agree nor Disagree	4 Agree	5 Strongly Agree			
CHALLENGING EMPLOYMENT ASSIGNMENTS AND OPPORTUNITIES				1	2	3	4	5

		1	2	3	4	5
14	Employees are offered more challenging work within the organization.					
15	Employees can work autonomously on their work assignments.					
16	Employees are skilled to do a number of different jobs, not just one particular job.					
17	Employees are given opportunities to learn new things.					
18	Employees are offered a good amount of variety in their job.					

Part B: ORGANISATIONAL FACTORS

5. How accurately do the following statements describe the effectiveness of your company's leadership practices at the organizational and the team level? Please respond using the same scale.

1	2	3	4	5				
Strongly Disagree	Disagree	Neither Agree nor Disagree	Agree	Strongly Agree				
	ORGANISATIONAL LEADERSHIP				1	2	3	4	5
19	The leadership practices in this organization help me to become a high performing employee.								
20	The leadership practices in this organization enhance my satisfaction with my job.								
21	The organizational leadership practices are consistent with my personal values.								
22	The organizational leadership practices make a positive contribution to the overall effectiveness of the organization.								
	TEAM RELATIONSHIP								
23	Team working is valued in this organization.								
24	Members of my team expect and maintain high standards of performance.								
25	Team leaders are recognized for promotion and development.								
26	Each member of my team has a clear idea of the group's goals.								

6. How accurately do the following statements best describe your company's culture and policies?

1	2	3	4	5				
Strongly Disagree	Disagree	Neither Agree nor Disagree	Agree	Strongly Agree				
	ORGANISATIONAL POLICIES				1	2	3	4	5
27	Organizational policies and procedures are helpful, well understood and up to date.								
28	Progress towards meeting planned objectives is periodically reviewed.								
29	The organizational structure facilitates the way we do things.								
30	This organization has a defined vision/mission to meet its goals.								

7. How accurately do the following statements describe your company's communication and consultation process?

1	2	3	4	5				
Strongly Disagree	Disagree	Neither Agree nor Disagree	Agree	Strongly Agree				
COMMUNICATION				1	2	3	4	5
31	This organization keeps employees well- informed on matters important to them.							
32	Sufficient effort is made to determine the thoughts and responses of people who work here.							
33	Communications across all levels in this organization tend to be good							
34	Organizational structure encourages horizontal and vertical communication.							
35	There is trust between employees and their supervisors/team leaders.							

8. How accurately do the following statements best describe your working environment?

1	2	3	4	5				
Strongly Disagree	Disagree	Neither Agree nor Disagree	Agree	Strongly Agree				
WORKING ENVIRONMENT				1	2	3	4	5
36	My working life balances with my family life.							
37	Overall this organization is a harmonious place to work.							
38	This organization regards welfare of its employees as its first priority.							
39	Workers and management get along in this Organization.							
40	For the work I do, the physical working conditions are very pleasant							
41	This organization offers a lot of security.							
42	A spirit of cooperation and teamwork exists.							

xvi

9. How accurately do the following statements describe your commitment to your organization?

1	2	3	4	5
Strongly Disagree	Disagree	Neither Agree nor Disagree	Agree	Strongly Agree

ORGANISATIONAL COMMITMENT	1	2	3	4	5
43	I feel a strong sense of belonging to this company.					
44	I could just as well be working for a different company if the type of work was similar.					
45	Often I find it difficult to agree with this company's policies on important matters relating to its employees.					
46	This company really inspires the very best in me in the way of job performance.					
47	I find that my values and this company's values are very similar					
48	There is little to be gained by sticking with this Company indefinitely.					
49	I am willing to put in a great deal more effort than normally expected to help this company be successful.					
50	I am proud to tell others that I am part of this company.					
51	I really care about the fate of this company.					

10. What are your plans for staying with this company?

1	2	3	4	5
Strongly Disagree	Disagree	Neither Agree nor Disagree	Agree	Strongly Agree

TURNOVER INTENTION	1	2	3	4	5
52	I plan to work at my present job for as long as possible.					
53	I will most certainly look for a new job in the near future.					
54	I plan to stay in this job for at least two to three years.					
55	I would hate to quit this job.					

56. In your opinion, what are the real problems that you observe regarding employee turnover management practices of your organization?

_____
_____
_____
_____
_____
_____
_____
_____
_____

57. Would you please suggest if there is anything to be changed with regard to the current employee retention management practice of your organization?

_____
_____
_____
_____

58. Any additional comments or suggestions

_____
_____
_____

Personal Data

1. Gender :   Male ☐   Female ☐

2. Your Age: 20-29 ☐   30-39 ☐   40-49 ☐   50 and above ☐

3. . Profession (Example: Management ...) _____

4. . Qualification : Diploma ☐   First degree ☐   Second and above degree ☐

5. Department: HR ☐   Marketing ☐   Supply ☐   Quality assurance ☐
   Finance ☐   Production ☐   Maintenance ☐

6 Experience (in years): 0-2 ☐   3-5 ☐   6-10 ☐   above 10 years ☐

End

Thank you very much for your participation.

Birhanu G.

Addis Ababa University
School of Commerce
Post graduate studies
Master of Art in Human Resource Management (MA HRM)

**An Examination of Employee Retention Management practices:
A Case study in Dashen Brewery PLC**

Part B

Questionnaire for
Focus Group Discussion (FGD)

By: Birhanu G/Silassie

Advisor: Wubshet Bekalu (PhD)

Focus Group Discussion

(Questionnaire to FGD)

Dear respondent(s),

I would like to thank for your earnest cooperation to participate in the focus Group Discussion (FGD). Without your cooperation it will be very difficult even impossible to conduct this discussion. The main objective of this discussion is to conduct a case study on employee retention management practices of Dashen Brewery. All the information collected will be analyzed confidentially and will not be disclosed to any other third party.

Attendance

Place: _____
Time: start_____
      Ending _____

Name of participants'   from which department

1._____ _____
2._____ _____
3._____ _____
4._____ _____
5._____ _____
6._____ _____
7._____ _____
8._____ _____
9._____ _____
10._____ _____
11._____ _____
12._____ _____

Discussion Questions

1. Does your company adopt one standardized human resource practice for every employee within the firm (a holistic approach) or apply differential HR practices for different types of employees? (e.g. core vs. noncore)

2. To what extent your company's **hiring practices** influence the retention of employees. State the type of performance measure/s used to test the effectiveness of the hiring practices.

3. To what extent your company's **performance Management** practices influence the retention of your employees.

4. To what extent your company's **training and career development practices** influence the retention of your employees.

5. To what extent your company's **succession planning program** influences the retention of your employees.

6. To what extent your company's **pay practices** influence the retention of your employees

7. To what extent your company's **leadership practices** influence the retention of your employees.

8. How do you communicate the employee's performance Results your Company?

9. . What are the major problems that Dashen brewery is facing with respect to employee turnover management?

Close the session with

Thanks

Aannex B: SPSS out puts

Correlations

		Org_fit	Rew_rec	Train_Car_devt	Challenge_ass	Org_leader	Team_rel	Org_policy	Commun	Wprk_envt
Org_fit	Pearson Correlation	1	.277**	.146*	.156*	.239**	.357**	.036	-.071	.282**
	Sig. (2-tailed)		.000	.042	.030	.001	.000	.621	.325	.000
Rew_rec	Pearson Correlation	.277**	1	.711**	.255**	.730**	.569**	.419**	.443**	.452**
	Sig. (2-tailed)	.000		.000	.000	.000	.000	.000	.000	.000
Train_Car_devt	Pearson Correlation	.146*	.711**	1	.378**	.784**	.509**	.510**	.486**	.522**
	Sig. (2-tailed)	.042	.000		.000	.000	.000	.000	.000	.000
Challenge_ass	Pearson Correlation	.156*	.255**	.378**	1	.403**	.474**	.259**	.289**	.274**
	Sig. (2-tailed)	.030	.000	.000		.000	.000	.000	.000	.000
Org_leader	Pearson Correlation	.239**	.730**	.784**	.403**	1	.571**	.544**	.483**	.614**
	Sig. (2-tailed)	.001	.000	.000	.000		.000	.000	.000	.000
Team_rel	Pearson Correlation	.357**	.569**	.509**	.474**	.571**	1	.337**	.182*	.332**
	Sig. (2-tailed)	.000	.000	.000	.000	.000		.000	.011	.000
Org_policy	Pearson Correlation	.036	.419**	.510**	.259**	.544**	.337**	1	.598**	.287**
	Sig. (2-tailed)	.621	.000	.000	.000	.000	.000		.000	.000
Commun	Pearson Correlation	-.071	.443**	.486**	.289**	.483**	.182*	.598**	1	-.051
	Sig. (2-tailed)	.325	.000	.000	.000	.000	.011	.000		.477
Wprk_envt	Pearson Correlation	.282**	.452**	.522**	.274**	.614**	.332**	.287**	-.051	1
	Sig. (2-tailed)	.000	.000	.000	.000	.000	.000	.000	.477	
Ora_commitement	Pearson Correlation	.186**	.222**	.209**	.171*	.265**	.233**	.444**	.316**	.136
	Sig. (2-tailed)	.010	.002	.003	.017	.000	.001	.000	.000	.059

Turn_inten	Pearson Correlation	.239**	.351**	.371**	.219**	.515**	.016	.224**	.298**	.503**
	Sig. (2-tailed)	.001	.000	.000	.002	.000	.825	.002	.000	.000

Descriptive Statistics

	N	Minimum	Maximum	Skewness		Kurtosis	
	Statistic	Statistic	Statistic	Statistic	Std. Error	Statistic	Std. Error
This organization has the same values as I do with regard to concern for others.	74	2	5	-.122	.175	-.722	.347
This organization does not have the same value as I do with regard to fairness.	74	2	5	-.237	.175	-.586	.347
This organization has the same values as I do with regard to honesty.	74	2	5	-.008	.175	-.859	.347
I feel that my personal values are a good fit with this organizational culture.	74	2	5	-.279	.175	-1.082	.347
Employees are given positive recognition when they produce high quality work	74	1	5	-.449	.175	-.757	.347
This organization pays well.	74	1	5	-.633	.175	-.962	.347
This organization offers a good benefits package compared to other organizations.	74	1	5	-.228	.175	-1.247	.347
This organization values individual excellence over teamwork.	74	1	5	-.042	.175	-.974	.347
This organization offers good opportunities for Promotion.	74	1	5	.061	.175	-1.170	.347
People are properly orientated and trained upon joining this organization.	74	1	5	-.247	.175	-.802	.347
This organization does provide regular opportunities for personal and career development	74	1	5	-.222	.175	-1.159	.347
Innovation and creativity are encouraged here.	74	1	5	.001	.175	-1.107	.347
The organization has career development activities to help an employee identify/ improve abilities, goals, strengths & weaknesses.	74	1	5	.003	.175	-1.310	.347
Employees are offered more challenging work within the organization.	74	1	5	-.741	.175	.010	.347
Employees can work autonomously on their work assignments.	74	1	5	-.556	.175	-.730	.347
Employees are skilled to do a number of different jobs, not just one particular job.	74	1	5	-.257	.175	-1.074	.347
Employees are given opportunities to learn new things.	74	1	5	.375	.175	-1.054	.347

xxiii

Employees are offered a good amount of variety in their job.	74	1	5	-.284	.175	-.693	.347
The leadership practices in this organization help me to become a high performing employee.	74	1	5	-.202	.175	-1.362	.347
The leadership practices in this organization enhance my satisfaction with my job.	74	1	5	.014	.175	-1.090	.347
The organizational leadership practices are consistent with my personal values.	74	1	5	.143	.175	-.816	.347
The organizational leadership practices make a positive contribution to the overall effectiveness of the organization.	74	1	5	.166	.175	-1.392	.347
Team working is valued in this organization.	74	1	5	-.471	.175	-1.098	.347
Members of my team expect and maintain high standards of performance.	74	1	5	-.562	.175	-.570	.347
Team leaders are recognized for promotion and development.	74	1	5	-.058	.175	-.988	.347
Each member of my team has a clear idea of the group's goals.	74	1	5	-.376	.175	-.461	.347
Organizational policies and procedures are helpful, well understood and up to date.	74	1	5	-.638	.175	.080	.347
Progress towards meeting planned objectives is periodically reviewed.	74	1	5	-.199	.175	-1.006	.347
The organizational structure facilitates the way we do things.	74	1	5	-.695	.175	-.417	.347
This organization has a defined vision/mission to meet its goals.	74	1	5	-1.005	.175	.304	.347
This organization keeps employees well-informed on matters important to them.	74	1	5	-.379	.175	-1.113	.347
Sufficient effort is made to determine the thoughts and responses of people who work here.	74	1	5	-.278	.175	-1.092	.347
Communications across all levels in this organization tend to be good	74	1	5	-.184	.175	-1.408	.347
Organizational structure encourages horizontal and vertical communication.	74	1	5	-.359	.175	-1.298	.347
There is trust between employees and their supervisors/team leaders.	74	1	5	-.343	.175	-1.013	.347
My working life balances with my family life.	74	1	5	.008	.175	-1.236	.347
Overall this organization is a harmonious place to work.	74	1	5	-.331	.175	-.627	.347
This organization regards welfare of its employees as its first priority.	74	1	5	-.128	.175	-1.133	.347
Workers and management get along in this Organization.	74	1	5	-.057	.175	-1.125	.347
For the work I do, the physical working conditions are very pleasant	74	1	5	-.678	.175	-.056	.347

xxiv

This organization offers a lot of security.	74	1	5	-.615	.175	-.492	.347
A spirit of cooperation and teamwork exists.	74	1	5	-.507	.175	-.871	.347
I feel a strong sense of belonging to this company.	74	1	5	-1.106	.175	.641	.348
I could just as well be working for a different company if the type of work was similar.	74	1	5	-.063	.175	-1.019	.347
Often I find it difficult to agree with this company's policies on important matters relating to its employees.	74	1	5	.186	.175	-.955	.347
This company really inspires the very best in me in the way of job performance.	74	1	5	-.545	.175	-.664	.347
I find that my values and this company's values are very similar.	74	1	5	-.132	.175	-1.117	.347
There is little to be gained by sticking with this Company indefinitely	74	1	5	-.143	.175	-.943	.347
I am willing to put in a great deal more effort than normally expected to help this company be successful.	74	3	5	-.574	.175	-.581	.347
I am proud to tell others that I am part of this company	74	2	5	-1.033	.175	.127	.347
I really care about the fate of this company	74	1	5	-1.848	.175	3.975	.347
I plan to work at my present job for as long as possible	74	1	5	-.346	.175	-.975	.347
I will most certainly look for a new job in the near future	74	1	5	-.412	.175	-.945	.347
I plan to stay in this job for at least two to three years.	74	1	5	-.404	.175	-.725	.347
I would hate to quit this job	74	1	5	.044	.175	-1.251	.347
Valid N (listwise)	73						

Regression

Model Summary[b]

Model	R	R Square	Adjusted R Square	Std. Error of the Estimate
1	.283[a]	.080	.061	.42599

a. Predictors: (Constant), Challenge_ass, Org_fit, Rew_rec, Train_Car_devt
b. Dependent Variable: Ora_commitement

ANOVA[b]

Model		Sum of Squares	df	Mean Square	F	Sig.
1	Regression	2.990	4	.748	4.120	.003[a]
	Residual	34.298	189	.181		
	Total	37.288	193			

a. Predictors: (Constant), Challenge_ass, Org_fit, Rew_rec, Train_Car_devt
b. Dependent Variable: Ora_commitement

Coefficients[a]

Model		Unstandardized Coefficients		Standardized Coefficients	T	Sig.
		B	Std. Error	Beta		
1	(Constant)	2.840	.223		12.759	.000
	Org_fit	.100	.056	.130	1.778	.077
	Rew_rec	.057	.056	.105	1.019	.310
	Train_Car_devt	.038	.049	.081	.775	.439
	Challenge_ass	.054	.044	.093	1.224	.222

a. Dependent Variable: Ora_commitement

Residuals Statistics[a]

	Minimum	Maximum	Mean	Std. Deviation	N
Predicted Value	3.3788	3.9763	3.6564	.12447	194
Residual	-.64300	1.25036	.00000	.42155	194
Std. Predicted Value	-2.230	2.571	.000	1.000	194
Std. Residual	-1.509	2.935	.000	.990	194

a. Dependent Variable: Ora_commitement

Model Summary[b]

Model	R	R Square	Adjusted R Square	Std. Error of the Estimate
1	.461[a]	.212	.192	.39522

a. Predictors: (Constant), Wprk_envt, Commun, Team_rel, Org_policy, Org_leader
b. Dependent Variable: Ora_commitement

ANOVA[b]

Model		Sum of Squares	df	Mean Square	F	Sig.
1	Regression	7.923	5	1.585	10.145	.000[a]
	Residual	29.365	188	.156		
	Total	37.288	193			

a. Predictors: (Constant), Wprk_envt, Commun, Team_rel, Org_policy, Org_leader
b. Dependent Variable: Ora_commitement

Coefficients[a]

Model		Unstandardized Coefficients		Standardized Coefficients	t	Sig.
		B	Std. Error	Beta		
1	(Constant)	2.494	.193		12.923	.000
	Org_leader	-.040	.048	-.104	-.842	.401
	Team_rel	.070	.045	.126	1.566	.119
	Org_policy	.213	.052	.364	4.073	.000
	Commun	.058	.046	.128	1.281	.202
	Wprk_envt	.021	.035	.059	.607	.545

a. Dependent Variable: Ora_commitement

Residuals Statistics^a

	Minimum	Maximum	Mean	Std. Deviation	N
Predicted Value	3.2611	4.0759	3.6564	.20261	194
Residual	-.65923	1.38869	.00000	.39006	194
Std. Predicted Value	-1.951	2.071	.000	1.000	194
Std. Residual	-1.668	3.514	.000	.987	194

a. Dependent Variable: Ora_commitement

Model Summary^b

Model	R	R Square	Adjusted R Square	Std. Error of the Estimate
1	.686^a	.471	.457	.38442

a. Predictors: (Constant), Wprk_envt, Commun, Team_rel, Org_policy, Org_leader
b. Dependent Variable: Turn_inten

ANOVA^b

Model		Sum of Squares	df	Mean Square	F	Sig.
1	Regression	24.761	5	4.952	33.511	.000^a
	Residual	27.782	188	.148		
	Total	52.543	193			

a. Predictors: (Constant), Wprk_envt, Commun, Team_rel, Org_policy, Org_leader
b. Dependent Variable: Turn_inten

Coefficients^a

Model		Unstandardized Coefficients		Standardized Coefficients	t	Sig.
		B	Std. Error	Beta		
1	(Constant)	2.792	.188		14.877	.000
	Org_leader	.182	.046	.396	3.918	.000
	Team_rel	-.231	.043	-.352	-5.320	.000
	Org_policy	-.125	.051	-.180	-2.456	.015
	Commun	.163	.044	.301	3.667	.000
	Wprk_envt	.189	.034	.444	5.533	.000

a. Dependent Variable: Turn_inten

Annex C: Training Needs assessment format

Dashen brewery PLC

Training Needs assessment format

Name: _____

Dept: _____ Section/Division: _____ Qualification: _____

_____

Training Plan for Period of:_____

Required Skill, Knowledge, or Ability	Priority Rank (1 = Immediate Need, 2 = Within 3 months, 3 = Within 6 months, 4 = Within 9 months,&,5 = Within 12 months)	Estimated Cost (If known)	Remark

Note: The supervisor should discuss training and development activities with the employee and then outline a plan for the employee to complete these activities during the next fiscal year. The employee and supervisor should understand that the implementation of this proposed training plan is contingent on the availability of funds and may be subject to additional management approvals.

Employee's Signature_____ Date_____ Supervisor's Signature_____ Date_____

Approval by the General Manager

_____

_____ .

Annex D: Exist interview format

Dashen Brewery Plc

EXIT INTERVIEW QUESTIONNAIRE

Name:_____ Dept:_____

Date of Commencement:_____ Date of Leaving:_____

Current Post:_____ Line Manager:_____

The Job

What is your reason for leaving? (Use✓)

Age Retrial		No Promotion		Accommodation	
Pressure of Work		Job Content		Pregnancy	
New Job		Earnings		*Care for dependents*	
Redundancy		*Working hour*		Moving Home	
Fixed term Contract		*Working condition*		Travel Problems	
Working Relationships		*Future training*		*Others*	

Other reason, please specify:

If you have a New Job, Where:

If you are taking up alternative employment, which of the following factors were highly influential to your decision: (please circle as many as you wish)

Basic Salary Domestic situation Additional Benefits Work/life balance Terms of Employment	Location Work Conditions/equipment facilities Discrimination/harassment Management Styles	Lack of Development Promotion prospects Other: *(please specify)* ....

xxx

```
..............................
...................
```

Is the current job description accurate? Do you have any suggestions regarding the nature of the job itself?

How do you feel about training you received? Did it improve your career prospects?

Supervision and Management

Did your Line Manager	Always	Usually	Seldom	Never
Show fair treatment				
Give praise for work well done				
Give encouragement and help when needed				
Explain the job properly				
Listen to suggestions/criticisms				
Comments				

What were your working relationships with your colleagues?

What was morale like in your department? Why?

How do you feel about the pay and benefits/facilities and services provided?

	Very Good	Good	Fair	Poor	N/A
Pay for your job					
Holidays					
Sick pay					
Pension scheme					
Office accommodation and equipment					
Meal & refreshment facilities					

xxxi

~~Sports & social facilities~~ Parking facilities					
Communication within the Board					
Communication within your Department					
Comments					

What did you like most/least about your job and why?

Is there anything which would make/could have made you stay?

Any other comments

Exit Interviews – Additional Tips

- Someone other than the immediate supervisor or second-level manager should conduct the exit interview. Often the interviewer is from the human resources department, but only if they are regarded as neutral, unbiased and trusted. Although a rather costly alternative, sometimes organizations hire outside consultants to conduct exit interviews.

- Interviewers should be skillful, well trained and good listeners. The interviewer(s) should use a standard format for the interview, but be flexible enough to ask probing questions. Some employees may initially give a superficial reason for leaving (e.g., more advancement opportunities or better pay) and only disclose the more important underlying reasons when probed. The interviewer should set a positive and relaxed tone for the meeting and use active listening skills. When dealing with a negative or critical employee, it is important to avoid the temptation to defend the agency or justify its actions.

- When using the exit interview process, particularly when several interviewers are used in different locations, it is critically important to document the results of the interview in a standard format so that the results can be aggregated into useful reports.
- Since the response rate from exit surveys is usually quite low, several techniques can be used to encourage the employee to respond.
- Your agency can schedule time for the departing employee to meet with an agency representative (perhaps someone from human resources) to turn in keys, ID cards, etc. and also fill out the exit survey. The survey can be completed anonymously and sealed in an envelope to be opened only by the person who compiles results.
- If the employee takes the survey to be completed at a later time, provide a stamped, self-addressed envelope.
- If the survey is completed online, typically the employee is given a password that provides access to the survey document. Permitting the employee to access the site from home for up to 30 days after departure may be helpful. In that time, you can use email reminders.
- The survey document should have adequate space for written comments, and the instructions should encourage the employee to provide them.

– June, 2011 GC; Addis Ababa University, school of Commerce

Aannex E: Organizational Structures of Dashen Brewery PLC

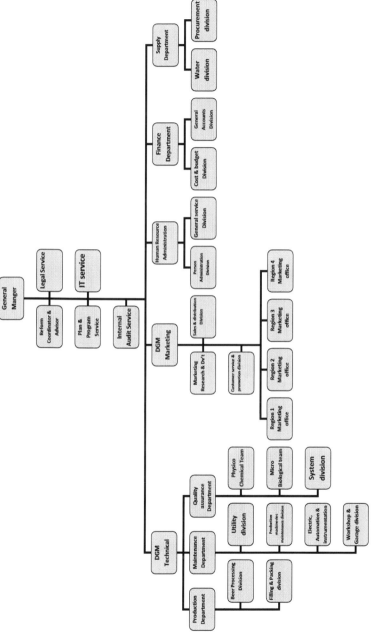

2560614R00070

Printed in Great Britain
by Amazon.co.uk, Ltd.,
Marston Gate.